Retirement Travels:
Postcards from Latin America

A whimsical series of journeys
to some faraway places

To my excellent cousin
Jean with love

Andrew Robinson.

Andrew Robinson

First printing: 2019
ISBN: 9781793126672

British Cataloguing Publication Data: A catalogue record of this book is available from The British Library.

Also available on Kindle.

Contents

Introduction

When I retired from boring financial services at the age of 64 it was not the end, but rather just the beginning. Suddenly my wife Jilly and I were free to explore the faraway places we'd always wanted to see, and we weren't restricted to two or three week breaks either; there was nothing to stop us from taking two or three months away, and better still we could time it so we escaped the miserable British winter.

The other big change was that for the rest of the year we could pursue the hobby we'd always enjoyed, gardening – but now we do it professionally on a part-time basis, and the money we earn pays for the lengthy holidays.

So from financial planning it was simple hop to holiday planning. With modern technology it's pretty easy to research the country we're interested in, make sure the weather will be good in January or February, decide where we want to stay, find the best air fares and book suitable accommodation. Our interests are wide ranging but include archaeology, history, nature study, fishing, snorkelling, walking, people watching and beach combing. Latin America ticks so many of these boxes, so it was a natural choice for us.

Instead of sending postcards to friends and family we could now send emails, and as I quite enjoy writing these became not only a way to communicate but also a record for ourselves. Gradually more and more people asked to be included in our emails, so it was a logical step to someday collate these virtual postcards into a book.

I hope you enjoy reading about our adventures in Latin America, and maybe feel inspired to do a little travelling yourself!

Part One:

Postcards from Mexico

Leaning Towers, Nudists and Giant Lizards

Our BA flight from London Gatwick was supposed to take nine hours but there was a ferocious headwind, so it actually took eleven – but at least we had a row of three seats to ourselves, so we could spread out.

When we arrived in Cancun we found that, because of our and other extended flights, the airport was absolutely jammed with people all trying to go through customs and immigration at the same time. It was another couple of hours before we finally got out of the airport and found our driver to take us the 35 minutes to our hotel, Acamaya Reef Cabanas in the little seaside town of Puerto Morelos. The only snag was he had no idea where it was! Fortunately, I'd spent so much time poring over Google Maps in the weeks before that I was able to direct him.

It was dark when we arrived, but lovely and warm, and we dragged our cases through thick white sand to our little cabin. Nothing fancy – rustic style with double bed, en suite bathroom, aircon and a fan – but it was right on the beach and we could hear the sound of the Caribbean gently breaking on the shore. I got a cold beer and Jilly made a cup of tea, and that was pretty much the end of a very long day.

Breakfast was supposed to be at 8am but the place was still tightly closed 20 minutes later and as we hadn't actually booked it, we decided to hike into town along the beach, which we were dying to see. Even at that time on a January morning the sun was strong, but we kept cool by letting the gentle waves lap over our feet as we walked, and greatly enjoyed the exercise after being cooped up in trains, planes and automobiles all of the previous day. And of course, there is something absolutely delicious about the very first day of your holiday, with the sun shining from a clear blue sky and everything to look forward to.

From our place to town was a 45-minute walk along a shore lined with huge all-inclusive hotels and posh villas. We were just passing yet another hotel when a bloke calmly walked down to the sea in front of us wearing nothing but a watch. I didn't think nudism was allowed on Mexican beaches, but this particular hotel seemed to be getting away with it. However, we did spot a sign that read: 'Sexual activity prohibited. Any kind of sexual activity in this area is strictly forbidden and will be sanctioned.' Which begs the question: what kind of sanction?

Shortly after, we came to a bar/restaurant on the beach and ordered a ham and cheese omelette each, which came with that classic Mexican favourite, refried beans. They're really good actually, much tastier than they sound, and as usual in Mexico the portions were large. Including tea and coffee, our brunch came to £8.

We enjoyed ambling around the fishing port of Puerto Morelos. It's a sleepy little town and the local shopkeepers all say "Hello," or "Buenos dias," and gently invite you to come into their shop, but nobody's pushy. There's a famous lighthouse leaning at a gravity-defying, tipsy angle thanks to a 1980s hurricane, which makes for some hilarious photo opportunities. Maybe they should twin the town with Pisa...

Whilst in the town we bought some basic

provisions and then cheated and caught a taxi 'home' as it was really hot by this time.

We had a lazy afternoon on the beach after lunch and then in the evening I tried a bit of fishing, but the conditions were all wrong and I packed up after I lost my favourite lure when it got caught up on a buoy rope.

That night we tried to watch a film on the iPad, but we couldn't keep our eyes open. The time difference means Mexico is six hours behind the UK and it took us a few days to get back to something like a sensible bedtime as opposed to 6:30pm!

Next day we walked along the gorgeous beach into town again, past the naked bloke – but this time there was some compensation, as a group of naked ladies were playing volleyball in the grounds of the same hotel.

We took a bus to Tulum, where the remains of a Mayan settlement are perched right on top of the cliffs overlooking the spectacular aquamarine sea. We'd been to Tulum before, but we couldn't resist another visit as we were so close and it's so special. There are some stonking great iguanas loafing about, generally right on top of the ruined buildings, so they look like gargoyles from the ground. Some must be getting on for five feet long!

Talking of iguanas, to get to Tulum from the bus stop there's a 10-minute walk along a shady lane with a few restaurants and various people outside with tame iguanas on their shoulders. They earn a crust by getting tourists to pose with said iguanas – but this time we saw a man with something very different. He had a tiny lion cub in his arms, drinking milk from a baby's bottle! We were so amazed that we forgot to take a photo. I've no idea where the cub came from, although years later someone suggested that the cartel bosses often have fierce wild creatures around, such as lions and tigers, to bolster their 'tough guy' image. When they are arrested the wildlife has to go somewhere – maybe to a zoo or a private collector, or maybe to a random man in Tulum...!

On the way back we stopped at Playa del Carmen, where we'd stayed some years previously, but it seems to have changed somewhat for the worse in the intervening years. The beach was absolutely packed, with loud music blaring and people trying to sell sunbed rentals or entice you into beach bars. We ducked back onto the pedestrian-only 5th Avenue and found our favourite bar for a well-deserved drink (I always say that) – camomile tea for Jilly, and a margarita for me. To my surprise and delight two margaritas arrived as it was apparently Happy Hour. Delighted Hour, more like – and they were huge! We spent a very pleasant hour watching the endless flow of fascinating people walk by. All shapes and sizes, hippies and well-oiled cruise ship passengers, every type of attire from brief swimwear to folk dressed as

Mayan Indian warriors, unbelievable tattoos and piercings, families and couples of every persuasion and denomination. The great thing was, everybody seemed to be in good humour; we just love the people watching there.

We took a colectivo (shared taxi, usually a white mini bus) back to our ultra-quiet hotel and dined on fresh fruit and red wine under fantastic stars and with the ever-present sound of the waves. We also tried to watch the film again … and failed miserably!

Lost Lures, Beach Brides and Rusty Brakes

At dawn the following day, with the sun peeping over the horizon, I was fishing off the beach when I caught a nice big snapper of 4lbs or so. A few minutes later something bit through the steel trace I was using! I hooked and lost a third fish and finally landed a garfish, which has an eel-like body and a long beak of a mouth lined with razor-sharp teeth...! For lunch, Dennis, our obliging host, cooked the snapper and it made a great meal for two.

Later that morning I snorkelled out to the buoy where I'd lost my favourite lure and spotted it firmly stuck to the mooring rope. I couldn't pull it out, so I swam back to shore to get a knife. A little operation on the rope saw my prized possession back in my grasp and the rope not much the worse for wear. Hurrah!

We'd booked five nights at Acamaya Reef Cabanas and enjoyed our time there very much, particularly the long beach walks, when we watched the pelicans and cormorants fishing or drying their wings, with frigate birds effortlessly sailing around the blue sky and various types of vulture circling even higher. Sweet little sandpipers scuttled about on the water's edge and the seaweed tide wrack, only taking flight when we almost trod on them. The sea never gets too rough in Puerto Morelos because, only 500 yards out, is the Meso American reef; it's visible from the shore as a white line and the open sea breaks against the coral.

Beach weddings are a popular sport at the all-inclusive hotels, with floaty white canopies rigged up as makeshift altars and the guests sitting in rows of chairs, all dressed up and sweltering in the 30-degree heat; the only concession is the men's tuxedos are worn with short pants. We walked past one group of guests fanning themselves whilst waiting for the bride to appear, and when we walked back half an hour later she was only just tripping down the sandy aisle. Bet she was popular.

On our last day I hired a bike from Dennis that looked as though it was on its last legs, terminal rust and neglect being the likely causes of death. The back brake was non-existent, just a shapeless blob of rust, but the front brake worked. However, it only had two settings: off or full on. There was nothing in between the two, which meant that putting the brake on completely seized the front wheel, so I pedalled very slowly along the flat, shady lane into town to buy a few supplies and book bus tickets for the following day. In fact, the bike ride was remarkably relaxing provided you didn't touch the brake!

Next day we said goodbye to our sweet little cabin and took the bus to Playa del Carmen, which got us there much too soon for our connection, so we had time to enjoy a drink and do some more people watching.

The first-class bus to our next destination, the colonial Spanish city of Valladolid, was very luxurious and very cheap. Fierce aircon, huge comfy seats with lots of leg room, a bathroom (as the Americans call it, although I couldn't find the bath), and even a television. We watched a film during the hour-and-a-half ride to the city, which, like most cities in the Americas, is built on a grid pattern. This should make navigation a doddle, but as usual I got it wrong and off we set, towing our suitcases in the hot sun but in totally the wrong direction. Three blocks later I checked the map, realised my error and had a good swear. Back we went to the bus station and tried again. This time we got it right and found our next hotel, Aurora, which turned out to be a little oasis.

Pyramids, Sinkholes and Aprons

We loved Valladolid. It's full of knackered old Spanish colonial buildings around a leafy central plaza and at sunset, zillions of birds jostle for roosting space in the trees around the plaza, creating the most amazing row so you have to shout to be heard above them.

Dinner was a typical Yucatan dish consisting of pork or chicken wrapped in banana tree leaves and slow cooked in a slightly piquant sauce until really tender. It's called cochinita pibil – or cochinita pitiless, according to predictive texting! With wine and water, the bill came to £15.

Early next morning saw us waiting at the colectivo

stop for two more people in order to make up the numbers and keep the price low. Colectivos are normally multi-seated vans that leave as soon as they are full, but in this city they were beaten up old taxis, a bit scruffy and with tired suspension but still vaguely roadworthy. Our destination was the Mayan ruins at a place called Ek Balam and the drive took 30 minutes. Each of the Mayan sites seems to have its own distinctive character; this one was quite small but boasted a huge acropolis topped by a 32-metre high pyramid which you're allowed to climb. Of course, I did climb it: from the summit I could see the tops of the pyramids at Chichen Itza and Coba, way off in the distance above the flat, jungle-covered land.

Back in Valladolid we had a sandwich lunch and did a bit of sunbathing on the rooftop patio of our hotel. Then we took a walk around this small city to enjoy the architecture and the often-deafening Mexican music blasting out from loudspeakers outside shops. They do like their music, and so do we, but sometimes it's a trifle boisterous. This city is like Maya HQ, with the ladies still wearing traditional dress – although the blokes favour cowboy outfits: jeans, checked shirt and Stetson.

After dinner we made our way to the main square, or zocalo, where there is a centuries-old tradition of dancing under the stars on Sunday nights. Sure enough, they'd closed the street to traffic alongside the zocalo and a big live band was pumping out great Latino music whilst the locals strutted their stuff. We loved it, and spent ages soaking up the magical atmosphere in the warm night air.

It was particularly hot the next morning, so naturally, being British, we decided to go for a long walk to find the market. On the way we came across one of the cenotes that this part of Mexico is famous for. These are limestone sinkholes with a lake at the bottom and were considered sacred by the Mayans because they're pretty much the only source of water. There are no rivers in Yucatan, at least not above ground. Over time they've eaten through the limestone so now they're underground, and every now and then the roof of a subterranean river collapses to produce a cenote. People love to swim in them as the water is clear and cool. We peered down from the edge, marvelling at the trailing exposed roots of the surrounding trees at ground level as they sought the water, whilst people swam far below.

The market was the usual riot of colourful fruit and vegetables, with many that we didn't recognise, and there were aisles devoted to meat and fish and lots of clothing stalls. For some reason known only to her, Betty, Jilly's mother, had asked us to look out for an old-fashioned 1940s-type apron with cross-over waist ties, and what should we come across but the very thing. Would it be the right size? Always game for a laugh, I tried it on – much to the amusement of the stall holders, particularly when I camped it up a bit! The Mexicans have a great sense of humour, and slapstick is an international language, of course.

Fat Birds, Flamingos and Norte Winds

The town of Tizimin was our next port of call and the bus took an hour to get there. We then took a second bus to the coastal town of Río Lagartos, misnamed by the Spanish as, despite appearances, it isn't a river (Rio) and the creatures they saw there were not alligators (lagartos) but crocodiles – or so the guide book told me. Our motives for going there were that it would be a break from cities and the place is famous for its flamingos, or flamencos, as the Mexicans call them, but I think they're getting confused with the dance...

The moment we got off the bus we could smell the

sea and the fish, for this is predominantly a fishing harbour. We wheeled our cases 100 yards down to the waterfront where there were hundreds of fishing boats, with pelicans, cormorants, seagulls and razorbills perched on the ones that weren't occupied by fishermen. Up above were the ever-present frigate birds on the lookout for a free meal. Yep, this is birders' paradise.

Another 100 yards along the front took us to our next home, which offered a nice little palm-lined pool flanked by a few spacious and well-equipped rooms. As usual, there was an en suite, aircon, fan and a little patio area, and the price of £25 a night included a good breakfast of scrambled egg, fresh fruit, juice, toast and jam, and tea or coffee. We were right on the seafront, separated from the water by a dual carriageway, which was something of a joke because there was virtually no traffic – maybe one car every five minutes! The locals don't bother with silly things like lane discipline or lights at night, and pedestrians amble about in the middle of the road. There were only two restaurants and the second one closed at 6pm. Sleepy or what?

The people here were noticeably different to the little Mayans of Valladolid, who struggled to make five feet tall. Here they were a bigger breed of people with more Indian features, and just as friendly and polite.

Río Lagartos reminded us of a tropical version of

Fleetwood, Lancashire. No concessions towards tourism, fish discarded everywhere because they were so plentiful, and the seabirds so fat on all this easy living they could hardly fly. We watched lots of little boats coming in to land their catches, and every one was loaded to the gunnels with big fish of many different species, including many I didn't recognise at all. Floating in the sea off one wooden dock we saw the long-dead corpse of what had once been a magnificent tarpon that must have been eight feet long!

As you'd expect, fish dinners were very cheap and ultra-fresh, so we ate well during our two day stay there. Day one was spent exploring by foot. After we'd hiked to one end of the waterfront we found a gravel path cut through the dense mangrove forest, so we followed this for about a quarter of a mile to where it abruptly ended at a deserted church. Although it was firmly locked up, we peered in through a gap in the wooden wall to see pews and altar in good nick. It seemed reasonable to assume that it was in regular use, but for what purpose in such an isolated spot? Weddings, perhaps?

We took a boat trip that led us on a high-speed trip through the mangrove-lined waters, passing various herons and white ibis or egrets (now I'm guessing, we're no birders!) until eventually we emerged into a wide, shallow bay where there were about 15 pink flamingos. Apparently, there are thousands here during the summer, but we were glad to see the few winter residents. That evening at sunset they flew over the harbour in beautiful formation. You rarely see them flying directly overhead, and at first glance the front end looks exactly like the tail end; a strange sight indeed.

On the way back from our boat trip we did a bit of trolling using both my rods, and much to my disgust Jilly out-fished me (as usual) with two barracudas. I have to say, they were very small and personally I would have used them for live bait. What do you mean, sour grapes? Remember the favourite lure that got stuck in a buoy rope back in Puerto Morelos and was subsequently retrieved? Well, it hooked an ENORMOUS fish but after a fierce fight the line broke and there was no getting it back this time. Bad language ensued.

On our last night in Río Lagartos I heard someone splashing about in our pool at about two in the morning, and I thought how inconsiderate it was to make all that noise at that time of night. I was on the point of going out to complain when I dozed off again, which was perhaps just as well as it turned out to be not a drunken swimmer at all but a violent gale that had sprung up and was blowing the palm trees around to such an extent that they were thrashing the water! This was the infamous Norte, the northerly wind that sometimes blows in from the United States at this time of the year and cools things down.

However, as we were travelling again that morning it didn't bother us at all. I was glad we'd managed to get the boat trip in before the wind arrived, though.

Our next home was the big city of Merida, about three hours' bus ride away. We watched – or rather, I watched – a very violent film during the journey but infuriatingly we got to Merida just before the end and they kicked us off the bus! Jilly, of course, hated the film and spent the entire journey looking at the scenery and trying to block out the screams. I'll never understand women.

The Five Tenors, Crufts and Fancy Ruins

We got off the bus in Merida and set off, cases in tow, along narrow and congested pavements for the two-block walk to our hotel. The paving slabs were broken where vehicles had crushed them, and vendors' stalls along the way made it even more tricky to negotiate. At the next junction, jostled by millions of rush hour pedestrians and deafened by revving cars, traffic duty cops blowing whistles and devastatingly loud Latino music blasting from every other shop front, I decided that this would be a good spot to check the route. Just as well, as once again we'd set off in the wrong direction! Cue bad language, followed by a swift U-turn and a fairly fraught walk through the hot streets which eventually brought us to Hotel Dolores Alba. Stepping through the entrance takes you magically from frenetic, modern Merida into a tranquil oasis of calm and cool. It was very like the hotel we'd stayed at in Valladolid but much posher and bigger, with a good-sized pool, spacious patio area with tables and chairs for breakfast, and wide, colonnaded landings.

We dumped our luggage and set off to explore. The main plaza is surrounded by wonderful 16th century colonial buildings and there was live music in the form of The Five Tenors – but with a difference as, bizarrely, this lot were Chinese and they couldn't sing for toffee. Good band though, and an odd mixture of traditional Latino music coupled with some classical.

On Sundays the plaza and some of the surrounding roads are closed to motor traffic and it seems that everybody grabs the opportunity to cycle or walk around the area in relative peace. Bikes are available for rent and 1,2, 3 or 4 seaters are to be had. The grandest road in this city was modelled on Paris's Champs-Élysées and is lined with magnificent mansions owned by the fortunate few who'd made their millions from henequen, the fibre made from the agave plant which was made into rope to serve sailing ships, amongst other uses. This incredibly lucrative trade came to a grinding halt as soon as they invented nylon, but the mansions are still there. The avenue is a dual carriageway, but it is also closed to traffic on Sundays, and the road was full of bikers of all ages plus skateboarders, rollerbladers and anyone else travelling with wheels but no motor. Everybody and their dog, or so it seemed, was enjoying a stroll down the gorgeous avenue on their day off, and the pavements resembled Crufts. All thoroughbreds, you understand, even some of the dogs. We had a lovely time gawping at the ultra-posh pads and enjoying the jolly atmosphere. We found the people warm and welcoming, as we have throughout Mexico. And of course we had to stop at the odd watering hole.

Quite close to our hotel was Bar Lopez, with its saloon-style swing doors and signs forbidding women and children from entering. Nothing of the interior is visible from the street, but as you walk by your ears are assailed by deafening Mexican heavy rock music and the sound of men's voices raised in violent argument with each other. Gringos enter at their peril! I wanted to go in but was too scared. One night we saw a chap come hurtling out of there and stagger along the pavement in front of us. We kept a respectful distance behind him and then watched in horror as he decided to cross the road just as a large bus came roaring by, to which he was totally oblivious. I think it was only the slipstream of the bus that kept him from being flattened; he was spun round by the force of it but somehow kept on his feet. We've never seen anyone come so close to sudden death and be so blissfully unaware of it.

Next day we had an early start to catch the bus to the ruins in Uxmal. As I mentioned before, all the Mayan sites are wonderful and have their own distinctive style, but this was the fanciest we'd ever seen. I think it must have been the equivalent of the modern-day show home. We could just imagine the builders saying to prospective punters, "Well, sir, this is our finest jaguar motif and we can do three different sizes, but you must appreciate that there's a lot of work involved by the finest craftsmen, so they don't come cheap. We can offer you a special deal if you order more than 10, but you have to sign up tonight..." He must have had a receptive audience because whoever built the place ordered everything on the menu! The site is full of intricately worked carved stonework and some massive buildings; most impressive. We got the time wrong for the return bus, but it didn't matter that we'd missed it as there was a nice restaurant there, so we cooled off with a couple of beers in the dappled shade whilst we waited for the next one. It's a hard life.

That night we had another brilliant evening of free entertainment in the Grand Plaza, this time traditional Mayan dancing with maybe 40 dancers, mostly of the older generation yet performing the most intricate and energetic footwork, not unlike

Irish dancing but using arms too. They were accompanied by a great 10-piece band and we so enjoyed being able to watch all this under the warm night sky, surrounded by happy people.

The following morning, we joined a multi-national group of tourists for a free walking tour of the historic centre of Merida. We were astonished to learn that, when the Spaniards conquered the city in 1542 or thereabouts, what is now the huge Grand Plaza was once the site of a giant pyramid. And there were four more of them close by, long since abandoned by the Mayans. The Spanish couldn't believe their luck – here was a free source of pre-cut building stone just for the taking! They immediately went about demolishing the pyramids to build the cathedral and the adjoining palaces and mansions that we see today, leaving the flattened area to become the Grand Plaza. The other pyramids were also dismantled for building blocks, so now there are five main churches but no pyramids in the city. What a shame.

Tomorrow we're leaving for our fourth venue, the coastal city of Campeche.

Prince Charles, Bulwarks and Aliens

We fell in love with the little city of Campeche as soon as we arrived after a two-and-a-half-hour luxury bus ride. Now a World Heritage Site, Campeche has had a very troubled history, mainly due to raids by British pirates. Things came to a head when all the pirates – including the French and the Dutch – joined forces and completely trashed the city, murdering, raping, enslaving and of course stealing everything of value. The Spanish were so incensed that they built defensive walls around the city with mini forts spaced around them, and much of this remains to this day. The buildings within the walls are in a beautiful Spanish colonial style, painted in bright colours and without exception appear to be in pristine condition, so every street is crying out for a photo. Had this been Cornwall the place would have been full of artists, it's so photogenic. In addition, it's on the Gulf of Mexico and there's a long promenade with cycle tracks and footpaths alongside the sea. Prince Charles visited the city a year ago, so that may have prompted them to spruce up the place.

Because we'd booked five nights in Campeche, we'd gone a bit upmarket to ensure we'd be comfortable, and we weren't disappointed. Our room was 20 feet by 15 with two double beds and a nice en suite. Situated within the city walls and only five minutes' stroll to the main plaza, the place also had a sweet little pool which was great after a hot day's sightseeing. Our room had a Juliet balcony with a bird's eye view of the street and the cathedral spires peeping over the roofs three blocks away.

That evening we found a super restaurant with no frills but excellent food. Completely open to one side, the place was packed with locals as well as tourists, which is usually a good sign. Jilly had fish stuffed with oodles of big fat prawns and I opted for chicken casserole. Both were delicious, and the bill came to £18 for the two of us, including drinks. Feeling nice and full, we walked the few yards to the floodlit plaza for a first-class sound and light show cleverly projected against one of the colonial mansions bordering the square and depicting the history of Campeche. This was followed by an orchestral performance in the warm evening air, with a talented female singer taking part in some of it. The cathedral and the city walls, or baluartes (like bulwarks in English) as they are called, are illuminated at night which really adds to the charm, and of course there was no charge for all this entertainment.

Next day we walked the baluartes all the way around the historic centre, some parts of which we were able to climb to enjoy the views from the battlements. After lunch we did another massive hike to buy provisions, especially wine as for some strange reason none of the shops within the centre sold it and I was getting withdrawal symptoms. Eventually our search took us to Walmart, about two miles out of the centre, and there we were able to buy everything we needed, including some squid to use as bait that evening. The only trouble was we were so hot and tired after all that walking – and, by now, laden with heavy shopping – that we had to cheat and get a taxi 'home', but it only cost £1 so was well worth it.

Towards dusk we walked to the sea and fished off the promenade, catching a parrot fish and a crab. As we walked along the front we were shocked to see that this otherwise immaculate jewel of a city was pumping its raw sewage straight into the sea. Apart from the stink by the outfall we could see a wide area where the sea was a nasty milky colour. Talk about spoiling the ship for a ha'penny worth of tar. Bet they kept Charles well away from that section.

The next day we had yet another early start to catch the colectivo to the Mayan ruins at Edzna. We knew the colectivos left from a street near the market, which is huge and frenetic, but we kept going in the wrong direction despite lots of helpful advice from the locals. If only they didn't talk so fast, and in Spanish, too. No consideration. Anyway, we got there in the end and it was well worth the effort. Simply enormous, with lots of giant steps to climb in the hot sun in return for stunning views. The little Mayans today are so small, yet their ancient civilization built such whacking great steps. I'm still trying to work out the logic, but it's tempting to consider that maybe the steps weren't designed for Mayans; perhaps they were perfectly sized for larger ancient aliens...

Forts, Nuts and a Ménage à Trois

I bought some prawns from the vast, noisy and congested market, which we loved. They're for fishing bait, but it's hot and we have no fridge so how do we keep them fresh? Solution: leave them in their bag on the marble floor of our room and stick the aircon on its lowest setting. Jilly is not too thrilled with this ingenious plan and tells me she is going down to the pool: "I'm not staying in this freezer; I'm off!" It was only minus ten or so. I try to explain to her that the bait must come first but I can tell she's not convinced. Strange creatures, women.

On either side of Campeche's seaboard there are beautifully restored 18th century forts, both with moats and working drawbridges. The moats were lined with sharpened stakes and quicklime in their heyday, sort of the equivalent of a welcome home mat. We took a 30-peso taxi to the San Miguel fort and greatly enjoyed the small but fascinating museum there which houses some exquisite Mayan pottery and jade death masks. Then we went up the staircase to enjoy the views from the battlements, where there were lots of old cannons pointing at the sea far below.

When we'd had enough we walked down the steep hill back to the coastal road, pausing only to try and help some very lost Americans in a rental car. We tried to tell them that the road they were on was a one-way system and they were going the wrong way up it, but off they went anyway, only to reverse back a minute later, saying they had a feeling it might be one way ... how do they survive?

We flagged down a colectivo to get back to town, but we only just managed to squeeze in as it was packed, with standing room only. The clutch had seen better days and the driver was in a foul mood, so the ride was a series of violent jerks as the clutch bit. Then he'd stamp on the brakes and go around corners too fast. We were all thrown around but somehow arrived unscathed.

That evening we went down to the prom to enjoy some more sunset fishing with my nice cool prawns. We found a good place to fish well away from the sewage outfall. Behind us, sitting on a pile of rocks, was a famous statue of a lovelorn maiden gazing out to sea as she waited for her sailor lover to return from his voyage. I caught a puffer fish, which obligingly inflated itself for a photo before being released. Suddenly, a bride all in white appeared, together with the groom and a cameraman, and started doing a photo shoot nearby, using the setting sun as a romantic backdrop. Then they spotted the statue and incorporated that into the scene. However, they wanted yet more action. Next thing, the groom was boosting his bride up onto the rocks in her tight gown so she could pose beside the statue. She had a bit of a scramble getting back down, but made it safely, complete with high heels. I would have taken the shoes off and tucked the dress in my knickers, but then I'm a bloke.

Watching all this was great spectator sport, and best of all I could still fish with the line hooked around my sensitive fishing finger, but suddenly they started heading our way. "Habla Espanol?" the groom asked, to which I replied with a strong Wiltshire accent, "Si, pero solo cien palabras," ("Yes, but only a hundred words.") which caused them to snigger. Then he asked in fluent Spanish would I mind if they posed with my rod? "No problemo," I replied, so suddenly he was holding my rod (steady!) and she'd sidled up and I was thinking ménage à trois, but then he started gently but firmly nudging me away and I realised they just wanted the two of them in the picture. And after I'd sucked in my gut as well! At this point I was worried that if the big fish were to grab the bait this limp-wristed Mexican would have the rod wrenched out of his grasp and all would be lost, so I implored him to keep a tight grip on the rod. Pushed out of the frame, I could only watch as the photographer took shot after shot, but eventually even he had run out of ideas and they thanked us before disappearing into the sunset.

Soon after, a very pleasant Mexican gentleman turned up with excellent English and many fascinating stories to keep us amused. His name, he said, was Adrian (!). Apparently, he'd lost his wallet (Alert! Danger! Klaxons! Beware!) but he entertained us for half an hour and gave us lots of useful information without actually asking for any money, which was an interesting ploy. After a while he confessed that he was hungry and asked if we had anything with us to eat. I knew we had a bag of nuts with us (Asda's best) but Jilly said no so I kept shtum. Finally, he said goodnight and set off, but I called him back and asked him if I could give him a bit of money. He wasn't expecting five pesos – only kidding, I gave him a bit more than that as the entertainment was well worth it, but I was glad Jilly had kept quiet about the food in our bag. I'd already had to give up my rod and I didn't want to lose my nuts as well...

On our last day in Campeche we took a taxi to the other fort, which was famous for its great views. The fort itself was virtually the twin of the other one, but the views were certainly worth the £1 taxi fare. Having toured the fort and marvelled at the views of the sea and the city far below, we again walked down the long steep hill to the waterfront where we discovered a pretty little fishing harbour on an estuary with a fish market and blokes mending their nets. In the very hot sun we eventually found our way to the prom and enjoyed the long walk back towards our hotel.

There's a wee tram thingy in Campeche that takes tourists on a conducted tour around the city, so we jumped on this and saw all the bits we'd missed, although the blaring commentary was in rapid-fire Spanish only (is there another version?). My puny efforts at learning the language had been well rewarded on this holiday, as very few Mexicans seemed to speak English in our last three resorts.

Tomorrow we're off again heading for our final base, the island of Holbox.

Golf Carts, Mozzies
and Space to Romp

An 8am, a luxury coach took us the two-and-a-half hours back to Merida. Our intention was to take the 12-noon bus to Tizimin, but when we enquired we were told that the noon bus was a second class one, which meant it stopped at every little village en route, and would take four hours, whereas the 2pm bus was first class and took half the time. We opted for the latter but it left us with a few hours to kill and all our luggage to cart about. I walked around the block from the bus station looking for a suitable watering hole to while away the time, but they were all greasy spoon joints right on the street, with traffic belching fumes and blaring Latino rock music, so I went back to the bus station to report the bad news to Jilly.

Whilst I'd been on my reccy she'd had a brainwave. We took a taxi to a lovely courtyard restaurant we knew in the centre of the city for a long and leisurely lunch, enjoying a tranquil haven instead of the 'orrible bus station. To add to our enjoyment, a group of local senior citizens met at a nearby table and took it in turns to sing lovely Mexican songs, accompanied by a guitarist. After a couple of beers I was itching to give them 'House of the Rising Sun', which is pretty well the only tune I can play on a guitar, but Jilly, ever sensible, wouldn't let me, thank goodness.

Taxi back to 'orrible bus station and then a smooth two-hour ride to Tizimin. As we approached the town we could see some big black clouds looming, but we got there in the dry and then agreed a price of £40 for the two-hour ride to Chiquila, the port for Isla Holbox. We'd only been going for a few minutes when the heavens opened, but our driver knew his stuff and we got there safely, although we'd just missed the ferry, so we hired a panga (20-foot open boat with powerful outboard engine) to whizz over to the island in 30 minutes. The island has virtually no motor traffic except golf carts – even the taxis are golf carts – so we grabbed one to take us along the pale sand roads to our next and final home on this holiday.

This long narrow island is in the Gulf of Mexico and the water is a different colour to that of the Caribbean; various shades of jade green changing to turquoise depending on the weather and the time of day. The island is virtually a glorified sandbar with a mangrove-lined lagoon separating it from the Mexican mainland. The beaches facing the Gulf are of fine white sand and stretch for miles, gently shelving so you have to wade far out before it's deep enough to swim. It's ideal for little kids - and big kids like us who love to paddle along the shore, enjoying the warmth and the people watching. Isla Holbox is famous for its whale sharks, which congregate close inshore in the late summer months. Visitors get to swim with these gentle giants if they're lucky, but of course they were out of season during our visit in February. The sharks, not the visitors.

Just for a change we'd rented an apartment here, complete with roomy kitchen/diner with fridge, cooker and TV plus a very spacious bedroom (what a past client of mine used to refer to as 'lots of romping space') and an en suite with walk-in shower. Outside there was a covered sitting area with table and chairs, hammocks and a double bed suspended on ropes from a wooden frame (presumably for swingers...). Only two minutes' stroll to the beach – sand road, of course, so no need for shoes – and ten minutes' walk along the beach to the little town and the wooden pier. The original intention was that we would catch our own fish and cook them in the apartment, but initially this didn't quite work as planned.

Our first day on Isla Holbox was spent exploring the town, which is surprisingly big for a small island, but still with sand roads. It's very laid back, with people ambling about in bare feet; the only vehicles are golf carts and push bikes. We did a lot of beach walking and that evening, suitably glowing from a day in the sun, we went for dinner at a simple outdoor restaurant by the sea. They had red wine, so what could possibly go wrong? Well, quite a lot, actually. The meal took ages to prepare and a succession of the owner's kids ran in and out past us, so I ordered another glass of red. The waiter brought the bottle over to fill my glass, but the wine ran out after he'd poured an inch. Our meals finally turned up and mine wasn't too bad but Jilly's was not nice at all and she couldn't eat it. I asked for a wine refill and the waiter came over with a new bottle. I reminded him of the short measure last time, so he filled up the glass but when I tasted it, it was fizzy Lambrusco, which I hate, and that's all he had. Suffice it to say we didn't go back.

Heading east along the coast from our place was a river connecting the lagoon with the sea. The estuary was supposed to be good for fishing, so Jilly and I set off the next morning to try it. It's called Mosquito Point, and we'd been warned not to go there at dawn or dusk because of the bugs, so we set off mid-morning with a fishing rod, some water and a towel. The weather forecast indicated rain, but it looked so bright we didn't bother with waterproofs. After we'd been walking for an hour, we realised that in our haste to get cracking we hadn't put bug spray on and for about the first time on our holiday we weren't packing any either. You can probably guess the rest...

We got to the river a little later and spent a couple of hours flogging the water, hooking and losing two fish, but then the clouds started building up, so we decided to head back. Halfway home the rain came down in bucket loads, but fortunately we'd found shelter in a half completed new building. An hour later the rain stopped and the mosquitos came out in force! Furthermore, the sand road was flooded so we were trying to negotiate our way through these mini lakes whilst carrying our gear and trying to fight off swarms of ravenous mozzies. Boy, did we get bitten! Fancy heading off to Mosquito Point with no bug protection: we shouldn't be let out alone sometimes.

That evening we set off to do a bit of fishing off the wooden pier, but we'd only gone a few yards when Jilly, wearing flip flops, slipped on a wet surface and landed heavily on her bum. Shaken up a bit but otherwise with no major damage, she decided to go straight back to the apartment, but she insisted

I go fishing as planned. I did, and I caught loads of fish, but I felt so guilty and worried about Jilly that I packed up after an hour and went home, where I was greatly relieved to find her cheerful and cooking dinner.

We watched a bit of TV after dinner and stumbled across the first episode of 'Sex in the City', a series we'd never seen before. We were immediately hooked, but we never found that channel again!

All in all, our first couple of days on the island hadn't been too great, but hopefully things were bound to improve.

Snappers, Dolphins
and The Sound of Music

After a couple of unsettled days, the clouds disappeared and the days slipped effortlessly by in the 80-degree heat, dropping to a pleasant 72 at night. We walked on average something like four hours each day, exploring the beaches and the lanes in town, with their gaily coloured houses. Many of the older ones are built of clapboard under a thatched roof. We fished from the dock and the beach and one day we saw a fishing boat come in and offload a monstrous bull shark, maybe 300lbs or more.

We met a fisherman called Manuel who offered to take us out on his boat for three hours of fishing, after which he would make ceviche from the fish we caught so we could eat it super fresh. We agreed to meet at 8am next morning, but by then the wind had picked up so it was postponed until the following day. We again turned up as agreed but Manuel's brother told us that Manuel had had "mucho fiesta" so he wouldn't be taking us out, but another of his brothers would. I asked him how many brothers he had. "Ocho," (eight) he replied, and then, after a pause, "No television."

We whizzed out into the flat calm lagoon in Brother Number Three's panga and then drifted while we cast for sea trout with soft plastic lures. I caught two, and then we motored further out for half an hour before dropping anchor and using cut bait in a patch of sea which must have been crammed with fish, because we just couldn't go wrong. Mostly they were some kind of hard fighting snapper the skipper reckoned were good eating; the occasional big fish took the bait but were never landed, to my fury. El Capitan then started to prepare the ceviche in an old washing up bowl, which put us off a bit, but he took great care to fillet the fish, making sure there were no bones or skin as he cut them into small pieces before adding lime juice, chopped onions, coriander, garlic, chilli and mysterious spices. We'd never had ceviche before and, not being the most enthusiastic fish eater in the world, I was apprehensive about tasting what sounded to me like raw fish, but we felt obliged to try it as he'd gone to so much trouble. Once it was ready, we cautiously tried a bit. Next thing, we were scoffing it down like starving wolves, using Doritos as spoons. It was so delicious.

On the way back to harbour we came across a pod of three large dolphins who seemed as pleased to see us as we were to see them, and they played around the boat for ages. We were so entranced that we forgot to take photos until the skipper reminded us. We also came across a turtle or two, so all in all it was a beautiful day.

One morning we took a golf cart taxi (they're all painted bright yellow with TAXI and their cab number printed on the sides) to Punta Cocos at the western end of the island, where we found a deserted beach and calm water. Within five minutes of casting out I was into a hard fighting jack, and that morning caught a dozen more, with most going back but a few kept for lunch. After a five-kilometre hike back in the noon sun (mad dogs and Englishmen?) carrying fishing gear, fish, towels and water we decided to taxi both ways in future. We loved our mornings there. Jilly caught two remora fish one day – the long fish with a sucker on its back that you usually see stuck to the belly of a shark, hoping for leftovers. Talking to one local, he told us they hate catching remora if they're out in a boat as the fish invariably sticks itself to the underside of the boat on the way up and then it's the devil's own job to get them off!

The jack fish were good to eat with some fresh salad and crusty bread from the market. However, one of our fellow guests at Ca' Rita, where we were staying, was a chap from the Czech Republic who just happened to be a chef and we gave him a couple of fish. Next day he brought round a little plate with a portion of the fish which he'd cooked with pine kernels, lemon, rice and mango. The end result was very special, so he got more fish from us!

The two young men who ran Ca' Rita did a very professional and caring job. One day Gaetano, (French father, Italian mother), who spoke good English but with an Inspector Clouseau accent, came around to give us some little donuts they'd made to celebrate an Italian festival. Another day I couldn't find any soap in the apartment, so I went around to the office to ask him for some. "Soup? We don't make soup," he said, which cracked me up. It's all in the pronunciation. He also gave us a little jar of mango jam he'd made, which was delicious with fresh fruit and yoghurt at breakfast time – so he got some fish as well.

About ten minutes' walk along the beach from us we'd noticed a huge sandbank at low tide on our first day. We'd been told that you could walk along it all the way to Mosquito Point when the tide was out, but ever since then we'd somehow missed our opportunity to do this. On our last day we finally timed it right; it was a spring tide and as we got there we could see the sand bar exposed for miles running parallel to the shore. Off we set, splashing through the crystal clear, warm water to keep cool in the hot sun. We enjoyed picking up interesting shells, marvelling at the emerald green sparkling sea and watching the multiple bird species resting on the sand and shuffling reluctantly out of our path as we approached. Two hours later we came to the end of the bar and stopped for a breather before heading back as I was keen not to get cut off by the rising tide. We made it (just!) and felt our afternoon siesta was well justified. We definitely deserved a margarita or two.

That weekend happened to coincide with the annual carnival, and for three days there were groups of dancers in exotic costumes singing and dancing to live music. All free, of course. They would start at 3pm and keep going until late at night, moving around the island from beach to beach and around the town. All you had to do was follow the sound of music and you came to the fun!

Finally, we had to say goodbye to this great little island. Dawn saw us on the ferry back to the mainland, then a three-hour bus ride back to Cancun. We had hours to kill before our flight home, so rather than sit moping in the airport for all that time I'd identified a restaurant on the Caribbean that sounded nice. We took a taxi there only to discover that it was closed! But nothing daunted – well, maybe a bit – we found another place nearby and had a relaxing time enjoying a long lunch and a drink or two in the sun. Jilly did a bit of last-minute shopping, and then we took a taxi to the airport for a relatively painless flight back to Gatwick. The flight home was a night flight, so we both dozed for the nine hours it took and were fairly fresh when we got back to freezing England.

I hope these postcards have given you a taste of the many little adventures we've had. We loved this trip to Mexico. The people were so gentle, polite and helpful, and patient with my clumsy attempts at Spanish. The food was usually excellent and we were very impressed with their hygiene. In some restaurants, even the male waiters wore hairnets, which was a tad disconcerting at first, and on the deli counters the staff serving sliced ham or cheese looked as though they were in an operating theatre with hairnets, plastic gloves and even face masks. I still got the squits, though!

Part Two:

Postcards from Nicaragua

Dripping Forests, Ossum Cocktails and Breadless Bocadillos

We enjoyed our trip to Mexico so much that we decided to extend our scope of travel to Central America. Originally, we planned to visit Costa Rica but after doing lots of research it became apparent that Nicaragua has virtually everything Costa Rica has except for the crime and the traffic – and prices are considerably cheaper. There was no contest – Nicaragua, here we come!

Our son Dan and his lovely wife Helena were due to have a baby on 29 December, and as they have something of a reputation for being late, we deliberately allowed for this when we booked our flights to Nicaragua just in case the latest edition shared the 'late arrival' genes. Two days before our flight Helena went into hospital, but baby didn't actually arrive until the following afternoon. Talk about cutting it fine! Still, we were very lucky to get special dispensation to see baby Cameron when he was four hours old – and looking remarkably good for a new kid on the block.

Next morning we were off, and had a good flight with BA to Miami. We'd been dreading Miami airport as I'd made the mistake of reading the online reviews, which had uniformly condemned this airport as the worst in the world by far – and the most strident critics were the Americans themselves, so it wasn't just us whinging Brits. As it turned out we had no problems there at all, so I think maybe the authorities had taken notice of all the bad publicity and sorted themselves out just in time for us. Or maybe we were just fortunate. Whatever the reason, we got through (or should it be over?) the various hurdles and had time for a beer (for me) and a nice cup of tea (for Jilly) before our next flight to Managua, Nicaragua. That only took two and a half hours and after some easy formalities on arrival we were driven in a people carrier to our hotel in the city of Granada. We arrived there 24 hours after leaving home, so it was a bit of a long day.

Our hotel was great: two floors arranged around an enclosed patio and a pleasant swimming pool. Big room with balcony area and views of beautiful trees and shrubs, both on our patio and beyond. We saw hummingbirds zipping around between hovers, and various raptors circling above and weighing us up, no doubt. The hotel was about five minutes' amble from the historic city centre, with its fine cathedral and historic churches dating back to the Spanish invasion. Granada is allegedly one of the oldest Spanish cities in Central America, which is one of the reasons we wanted to start our holiday there, and we weren't disappointed. The city has had a chequered career, with earthquakes, wars, British pirate attacks and also a crazy American called William Walker. who conquered the city in eighteen-hundred-and-something and then tried to conquer neighbouring Costa Rica. He was defeated there and chased back to Granada, which he burnt out of spite, leaving a placard that read, 'Here was Granada'. Nice chap. He and his bunch of mercenaries then tried to conquer Honduras but failed there as well and he was duly executed. Shame...

Nicaragua is very volcanic, and close to Granada there's a volcano so high it has a cloud forest on the top. Clouds hang over the canopy and the moisture condenses on the trees before dripping down onto the ground. We went on a tour up there, travelling on 40% tracks in a 4-wheel drive vehicle to the summit, and then taking a lovely hike through the dripping forest, where bromeliads and orchids grow happily on the trees.

We spotted a sloth, a creature I've always wanted to see but they've always been too fast for me. Suddenly, as we came around the summit to the windy side, the forest ended and was replaced by dry scrubland and wonderful views over Granada and Lake Nicaragua (which is the largest lake in the country, something like 130 miles long by 60 wide). In fact, there are a number of microclimates on the volcano, which is still active, and every now and then we'd come to fumaroles and smell the 'bad egg' fumes.

We enjoyed ambling around Granada and especially loved the pavements in the city, which were composed of pretty patterned tiles in various colours. We also enjoyed peering through doorways at the wonderful patios within. One evening, Jilly spotted a particularly pretty one and we were admiring the tiled floors when a lady suddenly appeared from inside the house and said, "Can I help you?" Caught red-handed, we admitted being nosy and to our surprise she asked us if we'd like to look inside! It turned out she was an American who'd been looking to buy a home in Granada some 15 years ago but at that time there was nothing of interest for sale. Then she heard of an alcoholic doctor with eight wives – no wonder he was an alcoholic – who owned a house his wives wanted him to sell, but he was reluctant to do so. Our new friend approached the wives, who ganged up on their old man, sobered him up enough to sign the papers, and lo and behold the American lady had herself a home. She spent years doing it up and it really was beautiful, with planted atriums open to the sky and pre-Columbian artefacts scattered about the place.

We took a walk to La Forteleza (little fort), which dates back to the 18th century, but as it was a Sunday it was still closed at 10am when we arrived. There was a man sweeping the pavement outside a nearby hairdresser's, so I asked him in Spanglish if the fort would be open soon. He replied in machine gun Spanish, but I wasn't really listening as I suddenly realised he was a transvestite, complete with hot pants! I nodded wisely and thanked him before we set off to find the cemetery instead, where at least six Nicaraguan presidents are buried in vast mausoleums. On many of the humbler graves of the recently deceased were photos of their occupants. Morbid but fascinating.

On our first day in the city we wanted to let our nearest and dearest know that we'd arrived safely, but Gmail wanted to know the answers to security questions before it would let us in and wouldn't accept our answers for some reason. We thought we'd phone Paul, our son-in-law, who is the family IT expert, but my mobile didn't work so we bought a new one and found that didn't work either! So, for a couple of days we were without communication until we twigged that we could just go into a cyber cafe and make an international call for very little money. Within 24 hours Paul had solved the Gmail problem but a week later we still couldn't get our new mobile to work despite several visits to phone shops and many young people trying to sort it out. I think it might be going under the hammer – and I don't mean in the auction room.

There were some interesting guests in our hotel. When we first arrived, there was a group of loud American students in the lobby, with one girl in particular having a very loud conversation on her Blackberry thingy, shouting "...and I had some ossum, ossum, ossum cocktails!!" ('Awesome', if the joke doesn't quite work in writing!) After they left, we met a group of very jolly Nicaraguans of later years who were determined to have a good time, starting with breakfast, when one old boy started singing at the top of his voice whilst shaking a pair of maracas! Lots of laughing and shouting before they cleared off.

We walked down to the lakeside one day with the intention of having lunch there, as I'd read that the area was nicely planted, with trees and shrubs alongside meandering paths running adjacent to the lake shore and many fine restaurants to choose from. When we got there the lake looked like the Irish Sea on a bad day, with choppy brown water. It didn't seem to deter the locals though, many of whom were enjoying a swim, but most of the restaurants seemed to be either closed or empty. The whole place had a bit of a forlorn 'end of season' look about it despite the fact that January is considered high season.

We eventually spotted an occupied restaurant, so we sat down and ordered a cheese bocadillo (a sandwich on Spanish bread), as we didn't want to do our usual trick of pigging out at lunchtime and then having no appetite for dinner. The girl took our order and seemed to understand my Spanglish. A little later she returned with the beer I'd ordered but gave Jilly a bottle of water instead of the hot water she'd asked for, so she could make her camomile tea. I tried again to explain and she said, "Si!" and wandered off. Shortly after, a chap appeared from the kitchen and said the girl wasn't sure what I'd ordered. "Agua caliente," I told him, so off he went and came back with a cup of hot water, but then he said they hadn't actually got any cheese so would chicken be okay in our sandwich? "Fine," we said. Five minutes later, back he came to say that the chicken sandwich would come with plantain chips and salad - would that be ok? "Yes!" we said, by this time so hungry we could have eaten the table. Ten minutes later the cheese sandwich arrived: chicken, plantain chips and salad. No bread, no cheese, but otherwise exactly as we'd ordered.

On the subject of chicken, the next day we were

off to the Pacific Ocean for a seaside break from all this culture – and the plan was to take what was locally known as 'the chicken bus'…

Christ Statues, Petroglyphs
and The Chicken Bus

Next morning, we arrived at the bus stop, which was in the middle of a sprawling outdoor market. Two blokes immediately grabbed our cases and put them on top of the bus, which was an ancient, long since retired American school bus. Then they told us that the bus didn't leave for another hour, so we wandered around the market, which was absolute bedlam, very colourful and very crowded; we kept a tight grip on our valuables, just in case. Eventually we got back to the bus and bagged seats together, but more and more people piled on and the conductor made us all squeeze up so that three adults could occupy seats designed for two kids. Then we were treated to a steady supply of buskers and vendors selling food, drinks and fruit. Finally, the bus wheezed off and soon we were out of town, bowling along good roads through rich farmland and pleasantly planted verges. From the seat behind came the odd clucking noise – we were really on your actual chicken bus.

Sometime later we reached our destination with our hair standing on end from the draught through the open windows on the bus, and found our way to the Hotel Colonial, which was to be our home for the next four nights. The seaside town of San Juan del Sur is arranged around a crescent-shaped bay with rocky headlands at both ends. Like Rio de Janeiro, there is a whacking great statue of Christ with arms outstretched (a fellow angler?!) on top of one headland; the seafront is lined with bars and restaurants specialising in seafood. Surfing is the big draw here, with boats going out to the surfing beaches and lots of young people in wetsuits shouting "Ossum!" at the slightest provocation.

We took some lovely walks along the wide beach and I tried a bit of fishing with my trusty travel rod, initially without success. However, on the final evening I caught three stingrays from the beach near the rocks and very, very carefully unhooked and released them.

Jilly found an American-run yoga school and

enjoyed taking part in various classes for an hour before sunset each day. The instructress said she was 'ossum', of course.

We'd read about something called a petroglyph, which is a pre-Columbian carved rock with obscure meaning, and were keen to see one on this trip. We heard there was one allegedly within walking distance of town so off we set. The instructions on how to get there were a bit vague and nobody we asked seemed to know what we were talking about, so we just kept walking along a quiet lane through open country. Eventually, hot and sweaty, we arrived at a bar and stopped to refuel. The owner was a German who told us we'd gone the wrong way (surprise surprise) but we were too knackered to retrace our steps. After our drink, we discovered that we were close to 'our' beach and paddled back through the refreshing shallows.

Not yet daunted by our efforts, next day we had another go at finding the elusive petroglyph and set off again, this time following the German's instructions. After a while we ran out of road and started along a dirt track. We'd only gone a few yards when we literally had to stop because we were walking through the stickiest mud known to man. It was like trying to walk with divers' boots on, so again we had to admit defeat. We squelched back to the hotel, where there was a lovely garden planted with shrubs and trees and comfy chairs to sit and enjoy a drink.

Having enjoyed a restful time in San Juan del Sur, we were off to the island of Ometepe next, which consists of a figure-of-eight island with a perfectly conical volcano at each end – twin peaks, in effect.

Wide Cattle, Cowboys and a Big Green Puddle

We took the ferry to Ometepe, which for those into quiz nights is the largest island surrounded by fresh water in the world. It's set in the middle of the second largest lake in Central America and, many years ago, this lake was going to be part of the link between the Pacific and the Atlantic, but Panama got the vote in the end. Originally part of the Atlantic, thousands of years ago volcanic action cut the lake off from the sea. There are still crabs in the lake which have acclimatised to fresh water, and there are also bull sharks that were marooned. In fact, there used to be a shark-catching industry in the lake, but this stopped when catches dropped off.

The ferry trip was about an hour or so and then a quick cab ride took us to our home for the next three nights, a place called Charco Verde (green puddle). Our cabin was set about 15 feet from the sandy shore of the lake, and dappled shade was provided by some big old graceful trees whose branches drooped into the calm water. To our left was the Charco Verde itself, a lagoon surrounded by a nature reserve consisting of a huge variety of trees and mangroves. We had free access to a double kayak, and we spent some happy hours at the end of each day gently paddling along the edge of the lake where the larger trees reached down to the water. It was an excellent way of creeping up on wildlife without alarming them, and it also gave us a clear view of the canopy where we could see birds and monkeys high above. Wading in the shallows were many varieties of waterfowl, mostly members of the heron family but in all shapes and sizes. The howler monkeys would roar away at dawn and dusk, which made it very atmospheric, and the froggy chorus would also reach deafening proportions in the evening.

The restaurant there served great food and we got to know one young waiter, who was trying to learn English. After serving us our dinner he asked, "Can I get you anything else?" to which we answered, "No thank you," and he replied, "Don't be shy!" – which tickled us no end.

On our first night at Charco Verde a party of Americans sitting together in the restaurant started off the evening in quite a jolly mood. We guessed they were probably part of a church group, of which there were many in the country helping to build schools or hospitals for the Nicas (Nicaraguans). However, as the evening wore on they became more and more rowdy and we began to revise that theory. Eventually, one of them staggered over to us and apologised for any disturbance but explained that they were a non-sectarian bunch of volunteers who had just finished building a school in the middle of nowhere with no facilities and no booze, so they were now having a well-deserved break and enjoying access to hot showers and alcohol! Not many of them turned up for breakfast next morning...

We went for long walks along the quiet lanes and were easily pleased by the circling vultures overhead (we may be in our more mature years but we're not quite ready yet!) and tiny mimosa – sensitive plants whose leaves instantly folded when touched. The island is very fertile thanks to all the volcanic activity in the past, and cattle are big business, so it was common to see a bunch of cows being herded down to the lake to drink by cowboys on horses, many of them small boys riding barefoot, with no stirrups, and just a blanket for a saddle. Despite this, they could really ride – and they always had a smile for us and a "Hola!" which was nice.

We walked past a field with a few cows grazing in it but from a distance we could see there was something odd about their horns. As we got closer, we realised they each had a long, sturdy branch tied to their horns and at first we were puzzled about this. Then we spotted one trying to get out of the field, which was surrounded by light woodland. No fence was needed because the branch effectively made the cattle too wide to get through any gaps in the trees. Ingenious.

All too soon it was time for us to board the overnight ferry to take us to our next destination, the mighty Río San Juan.

Darby & Joan, Twitching
and Admiral Nelson

We had opted to take the night ferry right across Lake Nicaragua to the town of San Carlos, which is where the lake meets the Río San Juan that runs all the way down to the Caribbean and provides the border between Nicaragua and Costa Rica. We'd read that tourists have to go first class (four quid each!) and that we had the option of travelling in an enclosed communal cabin with icy aircon and TV blaring in Spanish all night, or out on deck in a deckchair. Speaking to some tourists who'd already done the trip, we gathered that the deckchair option was the better of the two but they warned us it would get cold, so we'd brought a couple of light blankets with us in preparation for the long night to come.

On the boat we duly hired our deckchairs and watched the locals heaving on board tons and tons of bananas by hand. Then we cast off and went through a brief rough patch before the water calmed down. Like Darby and Joan, we sat side by side in our deckchairs with our new blankets over us and enjoyed the cruise. Somehow, I resisted the temptation to knot a handkerchief and put it on my head. As the night wore on, we got cooler, but far-sighted Jilly had packed all our warm clothes in a small rucksack and kept it to hand, so we gradually put on more and more layers and kept warm. We dozed our way through the night, waking up when we occasionally put into little ports for brief visits to load or offload. The lake was calm and the sky was clear so we could watch some spectacular star displays in the unpolluted clear air. All in all, it was not a bad journey.

Shortly after dawn, we arrived at San Carlos and, rather to our surprise, we were met on the banks of the river we were yet to navigate by an enormous chap who represented the hotel we were due to stay at. We'd expected to have to make our own arrangements to board the public ferry that would take us the 40 miles down the river, but Luis took us to a little lock-up office a few yards from the port and there we waited until it was time to catch the ferry. He was a short, immensely broad man who didn't speak any English and was content to sit there in silence for the hour or so we had to wait. Eventually, he escorted us back to the port, bought tickets for us and made sure we and our luggage were safely on the boat, which was a nice touch.

The boat was about 60 feet long with two powerful outboard motors, and we roared off down the broad river, spotting white herons standing like sentries every 50 yards or so in the margins. The boat was packed with an interesting mix of locals and a few tourists. The locals had more of an Indian look to them, and everybody was speaking Spanish. There were quite a few locals wearing wellies and carrying machetes and, periodically, the boat would carefully nose into the bank to let a few off to work in the fields and perhaps take on a few who'd had enough.

After an hour and a half we finally reached our destination, Sabalos Lodge, with its own little dock and staff waiting to help us off and take care of our luggage. We went into the reception area, where we were offered a complimentary fruit juice whilst they took our passport details. Then we were led through beautifully planted gardens to our cabin, which was built almost entirely of local hardwoods and bamboo and was reached by a double flight of rustic steps. Called the Tarzan Cabin, inside it was gobsmackingly different. No walls at all to the front to take advantage of its spectacular position right on the edge of the river. There was a double bed within a mosquito net canopy, a spacious living area with settee and easy chairs, lots of plants in pots and a separate bathroom, all under a soaring thatched roof.

The river at this point was some 300 yards wide, fast flowing and relatively shallow, with a small island in the middle. On the island there were a couple of trees festooned with white herons, and we sat for ages just watching the eddies and ripples on the water, and the birds fishing. That evening, a disturbance in the water by the island turned out to be two otters having a fabulous game of chase in and out of the river, almost knocking an indignant wading heron off his feet as they charged around. Absolute magic. Just as the sun was setting a group of black birds flew into the same trees where the herons were perched, and the newcomers set up such a clamour as more and more of them swept in that eventually the herons couldn't stand the noise any more and fled. When the light had completely gone, the black birds stopped their racket and the frog, cicada and assorted insect chorus took over. We even saw a toucan just sitting in a tree. It was all wonderfully atmospheric.

We set off for dinner, both equipped with head torches, and immediately we spotted a huge frog at the bottom of our stairs and several more on the short walk to the restaurant. For some reason the lad who was waiting on us was wearing a sailor's cap reminiscent of the Pirates of Penzance musical. We asked him his name and he replied "Nelson". It seemed an odd choice of name for a young Nicaraguan.

Next day we'd booked a jungle hike with a guide, but before setting off we were asked to select a pair of wellies each from the vast stock held at the hotel. The reason soon became clear as the path through the jungle was extremely boggy and at times we both got a wee bit stuck, which made us laugh. We saw a host of wildlife in the jungle, including lines of leaf cutter ants, each one carrying a chunk of leaf, a column of soldier ants, spider monkeys and squirrels. Periodically, our guide would stop and explain the medicinal properties of certain trees, and before long it became apparent that there was no ailment known to man that some jungle plant couldn't cure. The only problem was, the guide kept flapping his cap and slapping himself as the mosquitos homed in on him. I was so tempted to ask which tree stopped bugs from biting, but eventually I took pity on him and offered him an anti-mosquito wet wipe, which solved the problem instantly.

After three hours we boarded a boat and whizzed further downstream to a very attractive little fort dating back to the 16th century, built by the Spanish to prevent pirates coming up the river and across the lake to pillage Granada. Henry Morgan and Nelson both had a go – Nelson's forces actually took the fort but had to retreat back to the Caribbean a couple of weeks later because the sailors were all dying of yellow fever, dysentery and malaria. Not many people know that, as Michael Caine might have said. And that explained why the young waiter was named after a British hero, perhaps. Anyway, back to the fort - they chose that spot to build it as there are fearsome rapids within sight just downstream, so any boats coming from the sea would be very vulnerable to cannon shot from the fort as they tried to manhandle their boats past the rapids. From our point of view, we were glad they did build it there as the view from the ramparts was spectacular.

We stopped for lunch at a riverside restaurant a few yards from the fort and had giant freshwater shrimps, which were the size and shape of small lobsters, just as delicious and cost about six quid for the two of us.

Curiously, we found everything we'd seen in the jungle also lived in the gardens of Sabalos Lodge and then some, including hummingbirds, scarlet and black birds, yellow birds, 18-inch long bright green lizards and even a crèche of young caiman in a backwater close to our cabin. Lots of howler monkeys too, so we were very happy there. Jilly found a riverside deck on which to do her yoga, and we slept like logs every night, lulled to sleep by the chuckling river below us.

We had access to a double seater kayak, but I said to the manageress that the river was too fast for kayaking unless you were happy just going downstream – we'd never be able to paddle back against that current. "No problemo!" she said, and they hauled the kayak up onto the 20-foot hotel launch and took us upstream to where a big, slow river joined the Río San Juan. There they offloaded the kayak; we got in and agreed to meet them a couple of hours later at the same spot. We gently paddled along, seeing turtles basking on half submerged logs and a variety of other interesting creatures, including women washing clothes in the river and little kids jumping in or fishing. It was all so peaceful and relaxing, with the temperature just right if you didn't paddle too hard.

One day we went for a walk across the fields to a nearby village and two of the hotel's dogs decided they'd come with us. One was a puppy Doberman called Mr Jingo, who was really loveable – and we never thought we'd say that about a Doberman. The other was an elderly yellow Labrador who got a bit hot; halfway there he flopped down in a very muddy puddle for a rest. The walk took us about an hour, and the dogs were still with us. We went into a bar for a drink and the Lab crashed out beside us for a snooze, leaving a very muddy imprint when we left. In my best Spanglish I tried to explain that the dogs didn't belong to us but I'm not sure the owners were convinced. Nobody there spoke English, even in the Lodge, so it was a good opportunity for me to practice my Spanish – with Jilly, as usual, translating their replies for me! She doesn't speak Spanish, but she says she just listens to them and watches their body language. I, on the other hand, am far too busy trying to formulate my next sentence to pay any attention to what anyone says in response! Personally, I think Jilly uses black magic...

Runaway Horses, Scorpions and Chewing Gum Change

With considerable regret, we left our Tarzan Cabin and boarded the 7.30am public boat. As we tore upstream, loud Latino music was played, which was great, and, as before, we made periodic bankside stops to drop off and pick up machete-wielding locals. Eventually we reached San Carlos, where box-shaped Luis was waiting for us with his enigmatic smile. Our bags were put on a handcart and we followed Luis as he waddled off to his strange lock-up office. We were running short of cash, so I explained that we needed to get to an ATM and he led the way. Before leaving England, we'd put our spending money into Thomas Cook Cash Passports, a type of pre-paid credit card, but the machine refused to take it. We tried other cards – no joy. We were beginning to feel quite anxious now. We trudged to another ATM – the only other one in town and our last hope – and Jilly managed to persuade it to part with some cash so we were rich again, at least for a few days.

Luis then marched us round to a restaurant with an open verandah and views across the port and the lake. To our surprise we had an included lunch, and whilst we were enjoying that a seaplane touched down on the lake so there was entertainment as well!

Lunch over, Luis then picked us up in a battered truck (a pickup truck?) and drove about a kilometre out of town before turning right at the airport sign. Immediately we were on a dirt track and after a short, bumpy ride we arrived at the airport, which consisted of a tin shed next to a dirt track runway with a snack kiosk alongside. We'd heard that the domestic airline, La Costena, was very strict on baggage weight and charged for anything over 30 kgs. They weighed our luggage, which we knew was well over the limit, and weighed us as well for good measure, but to our surprise they didn't charge us extra. That was the nearest we got to a security check. There was no X-ray machine and they weren't in the slightest bothered about the bottles of water we were carrying. In fact, we were then free to wander over to the kiosk and buy more liquids, where they gave me my change in the form of packets of chewing gum.

Suddenly the sleepy shack was awakened from its dozy state by high drama! There was no security fence around the airport and a white horse had appeared on the runway, with the plane due to arrive at any minute. The security men, who'd been having a nice rest until then, had to get up and try to drive the horse off the runway, but of course it perversely decided to stay put and it was gradually chased further and further down the track. At this point, enter stage left a lone cowboy, complete with Stetson and on horseback, presumably looking for his escaped steed. He trotted up to the edge of the runway, spotted the escapee way down the track and still being pursued by the security men, and wisely did a U-turn and disappeared. "Not my horse..."

In the fullness of time the white horse trotted back towards us and a taxi sprang into action, driving onto the runway to head off the horse, the driver banging the outside of his door and honking his horn. The horse was duly herded off the runway and a couple of minutes later the little plane roared in.

The plane held 12 people plus the co-pilot and the pilot, who was a pretty young girl. Most of us couldn't work out how our seatbelts worked but as there was no pre-flight instruction from the crew, we didn't bother with them. The single prop revved furiously and we lurched off along the dirt track. We saw the girl at the controls waving to her friends in the shack as we sped by, and somehow we took off and flew for some 40 minutes over the lake that had previously taken all night to cross by boat. After a soft landing at Managua airport (with real tarmac!), we took a taxi to our overnight hotel, which happened to be a casino as well and very posh indeed compared to the rustic paradise we'd just left. Posh it might have been, but as the porter opened the door of our room Jilly spotted a scorpion scuttling along the floor – which the porter casually stepped on! There we enjoyed our first hot shower for days, although I think Jilly missed my screaming as the cold water used to hit me, back at the Tarzan Cabin.

We swanned about in the lap of luxury that evening, had a good kip in a queen-sized bed and got up at 4.30am for our next flight to a tiny island in the Caribbean.

Drowned Rats, Coconuts
and Don King's Brother

We caught the 'big' plane (a 50-seater) bright and early and had a smooth flight to Bluefields, a little town on the Nicaraguan Caribbean coast, where a few people got off and a few more got on. I don't think they were the same people. Bluefields is named after a Dutch pirate called Bluefeld, and from now on we were heading for Pirates of the Caribbean territory. The plane took off again after 15 minutes and flew for another half hour before landing on the island of Big Corn, some 70 kms from the Nicaraguan mainland.

After a $3 taxi ride – via the only ATM on the

island, which again spat out our trusty Thomas Cook card – we took a tea break in the cafe next to the harbour whilst we waited for the panga to take us to Little Corn Island. There was a bit of a delay because the captain was playing football. The panga was an open boat, about 30 feet long, and it was packed with some 60 people. We'd read about the 10-mile journey from Big Corn to Little Corn and knew that it was usually a rough ride as it headed into the prevailing wind. We also knew that those in the front tended to get a lot of slamming but stayed fairly dry whilst those in the rear had a smoother ride but got soaked with spray. Like good Boy Scouts we were prepared, with dustbin liners to cover our bags and waterproof jackets to cover us, as we intended to sit in the stern. However, in all the confusion the cases were grabbed by the crew and stored away before we had time to cover them; our rucksacks containing the jackets were also stored away before we knew it. The best laid plans etcetera... Then followed a rollercoaster ride, with people in the bows screaming as the boat slammed down and those in the stern having buckets of warm sea water chucked over them, or so it seemed. People pay a lot of money for that sort of ride in theme parks, but for us it was only $5 each.

Forty minutes later, two drowned rats climbed off the boat at Little Corn harbour and were met by Henry, a smiling young local lad clutching a sign saying 'Mr Andrew' and a wheelbarrow. Our bags, which had somehow remained dry, were put into the barrow and we followed Henry through the village and along a path through the jungle, which took us along a sandy path to the other side of the island. After about twelve minutes we arrived at our home for the next eight nights, Little Corn Beach & Bungalow, or B & B for short. We'd had a bit of luck with the booking. It seemed that they'd made a cock up with our reservation and to compensate we'd been upgraded to a top of the range cabin. The down side was that we'd have to spend the first night in the communal bunkhouse, but they'd arranged things so we didn't have to share the bathroom and it was only us staying there; I think we got a good deal. We enjoyed a restful night's sleep until, at some point in the wee small hours, there was an almighty bang as a coconut crashed down onto the corrugated iron roof. Foul language ensued!

B & B consisted of about 12 cabins, each named after a shipwreck story, so there was a Robinson cabin next door to the Crusoe cabin and so on. We were in the Gulliver cabin, which, somewhat perversely, was huge. The first-floor bedroom, containing a comfy queen-size bed under a vast mosquito canopy and en suite bathroom, was reached via a bamboo ladder; beneath was a large seating area and a wide, covered decking area leading outside. Palm trees provided dappled shade and we were twenty paces from the amazing azure sea. Being on the windward side, there was always a refreshing breeze and the cabin had no glass in the windows, only bug-proof mesh, so it was delightfully airy.

We had mains electricity from 2pm until 5am, but the restaurant, only a few yards away, opened at 7am so we could get our vital morning tea and coffee fix. Hammocks and reclining chairs were scattered about amongst the palm trees and the food, as in nearly all our 'homes' across this country, was exceptionally good. Being American owned (B & B, not the country) the portions were gargantuan, so we generally shared a meal so we'd have room for the next one.

The staff were delightful; they were mostly islanders and generally of African heritage with a sprinkling of Indian, Spanish and European pirate blood, just to make things interesting. They called us Mr Andrew and Miss Jilly, which was sweet once you got used to it. One Spanish-speaking waitress used to call me Don Andres, which made me feel very grand! There were a number of resident dogs, all of them rescue dogs and all of them characters. Dixie had a face like a meerkat and an uncanny knack of knowing exactly when your meal was served; you soon became aware of a pair of patient brown eyes boring into you. Our favourite was My Son, who had an undershot jaw revealing all his lower teeth. Every time I saw him, I couldn't help remembering the little dog that used to say "Sausages!" on a TV show long ago. There was a parrot called Lola, who sat in a tree each morning where she'd chat away to herself. A bright green parrot with a big yellow blob on the back of her head, she looked so garish with her dayglo colours, but once she was in the tree it was a real job to spot her even though she might only be a foot away; she was brilliantly camouflaged. Literally.

The beach was about a mile of clean sand flanked by palm trees and the sea displayed every shade of blue you could imagine. The water was warm and we went for long walks splashing through the shallows to cool our feet as we went. Of course, this tiring and demanding work necessitated frequent stops at various watering holes to keep ourselves hydrated.

Little Corn Island is small and you can, in theory, walk from one end to the other in an hour along paths through the jungle, but as usual we often managed to start nattering and get lost as there were very few signposts. When we did spot a sign, it was usually painted on a rock and half covered in tropical undergrowth, but it didn't seem to matter; we always ended up on a beach and then we could get our bearings again.

On one such walk we came across a local with a machete, splitting coconuts. When he noticed us watching, he gave us a demonstration, taking the husk off the nut and slicing an opening in the shell so we could take a refreshing drink. He then showed us another coconut which was already sprouting and he split this open to reveal a spongy white centre that he invited us to taste. It was surprisingly sweet, a bit like candy floss. He gave us the rest of the nut to eat and wouldn't take any money; he was a typical friendly gentle islander.

On yet another walk, we came across an extraordinary beach resort owned by an eccentric artist/sculptor where there were amazing creations made from driftwood and whatever else was washed up on the beach. He'd even made an incredible windmill that looked like something from a Mad Max film. Sometimes we'd have whole beaches just to ourselves. It was like a storybook desert island.

At B & B there was a night watchman called Mr Toro who deserves a mention. Think of Don King's extrovert brother and you'll have a pretty good idea of what he looked like. With a mane of electrocuted white hair, a lined black face that looked as though it was carved from stone and a long white beard, he was apparently feared by the other islanders. It seems he made a point of telling the local likely lads that he didn't give a monkey's what they did elsewhere on the island but if they ever tried anything at B & B, he'd kill them – and they believed him. Imagine him patrolling the grounds with his guard dog, My Son, with his terrible jaw, and you have a pretty scary picture. Not that there was much crime here; we never felt at risk and all the islanders we met were kind and polite to us.

The only town of any sort on Little Corn is known as The Village; it's on the leeward side of the island so the water is always calm. We spotted huge tarpon fish rolling about on the surface just off the shore there. Visiting anglers – including me – tried catching them but the fish were far too smart, which was probably just as well as they'd have smashed my lightweight tackle for sure. There were a number of bars and restaurants along the front and it was pleasant to stroll along and take in the peaceful scene of brightly coloured fishing boats bobbing about, the local kids leaping off the dock into the calm, blue sea and the occasional burst of reggae music to remind us that we were well and truly on a Caribbean island, man.

Most of the locals speak Creole and Spanish or English, but of course there was no way of telling who spoke what. Usually when we approached someone we'd say "Hi," and they'd reply "Hola" – or we'd say "Hola" and they'd say "Hi". But by and large people don't pass each other without saying hello in whatever language, which is as it should be.

We went for a number of fishing trips and caught plenty, including barracuda, kingfish, Spanish mackerel, grunts (because they grunt when you land them), yellow snapper and trigger fish. The trigger fish has an interesting defence mechanism. When frightened or alarmed, it raises a fearsome spike by its dorsal fin. It was fascinating for me to see how my light fishing rod and artificial lures fared against the local skipper's tried and tested real fish baits. Invariably, mine caught more – which made me very chuffed. On one trip I caught one and a half kingfish. It would have been two, but something ferocious bit off the rear half of the second fish as I was reeling it in. Not very sporting, I thought.

The only trouble with all this lovely boat fishing was that I got a very sore bum from the hard seats and the constant rolling about in sometimes pretty hefty seas, so eventually I had to give it up for a while to recover!

We spotted tiny frogs and colourful butterflies on our hikes, and in the evening as the light was fading the path through the jungle from The Village was lit by thousands of fireflies. One day I saw what I thought was a discarded snakeskin in a low palm tree, so I gave it a tentative pull. To our dismay, the tail reacted – it belonged to a live snake! We traced the body in and out of the palm fronds looking for the head. It seemed to go on and on but at last we came to a tiny pointed head at the front end of a pencil-thin, six-foot-long body. We took a photo and showed it to the locals later, who told me it was a whip snake.

Our eight days whizzed by and all too soon we

had to face the inter-island panga joyride again, but this time we were better prepared. As the wind and waves were behind us on the return journey it proved to be much drier, but there was a lot of corkscrewing on a very overloaded boat and the skipper needed to be sharp on the steering and throttle to stop the boat from rolling over, so again it was an interesting ride. (Fast forward to 2018 and the same boat did actually capsize, with the loss of several lives.) Midway across, the boat stopped and a very large lady who was perched on a barrel of fuel had to be shifted so the fuel pipe could be switched from the empty barrel to the full one. Fortunately, nobody decided to light up during this operation or you wouldn't be reading this!

We were looking forward to returning to the final destination of our Nicaraguan adventure - Big Corn Island.

Breakdowns, Cruise Ships and Sybil Fawlty

Our new home on Big Corn was the Arenas Beach Resort, which was a pretty posh place by our usual standards. Situated on a magnificent mile-long beach with warm, shallow water, the sea was calm as we were once again on the lee side of the island. Along the broad beach, resort guests could relax in white pavilions containing luxurious L-shaped sofas under pitched roofs, with white net 'foils' (Jilly's word) to offer floaty sun protection in the late afternoon. The pale sand was absolutely pristine; no rubbish to be seen, no shells, no driftwood and sometimes no people other than us on this vast beach. But as with all picture postcard places, there were a couple of minus points. The road to the hotel and two other resorts further along the beach was the worst dirt track you ever did see, difficult even to walk along, let alone drive on, so the natural result was that the locals used the top section of the beach as their road instead. This wasn't a big problem as there were very few cars, but it was weird having to use the Green Cross Code on a tropical beach! The other negative was that when there was no wind, which was most days, the sand flies got hungry and Jilly in particular proved to be the meal of choice for the little bleeders, despite using bug repellent.

The sea colours changed constantly with the weather and the time of day. Most mornings would see me fishing off the beach at dawn with a flat calm sea, but an hour later a little welcome breeze would ripple the water as the sun rose above the palm trees, turning the sea various shades of blue to azure. At sunset we'd have an hour's fishing again and enjoy the changing light. Sometimes the sky would turn deep orange and reflect onto the ocean, and then, as the light was nearly gone, a strong fish would take the bait and everything was perfect. Well, it was for me. Not sure about the fish.

Every time I went fishing the locals sidled up, examined my fishing tackle, and told me it was too weak, the tide was wrong, my bait was wrong, it was the wrong time of day or the wind was in the wrong direction. Oh, and the fishing's better off the dock. I always nodded my complete understanding and thanked them for their well-meaning advice, but sometimes I had great success despite all the gloom and doom, mainly with a super strong fish called bonefish which goes off like a rocket on light tackle. I also caught a sand shark off the much-vaunted dock – but it was only four inches long!

Part of our hotel's beach frontage included a big old wooden boat under a white canopy, which was signposted 'Boat Bar', but it was only used on special occasions. One such occasion arose whilst we were there when a splendid tall ship appeared in the bay and anchored about a mile offshore. We were told it was a luxury cruise ship for older folk, and as part of their schedule the passengers were to be ferried over to the hotel to have a boozy lunch at the Boat Bar. The hotel staff carried crate after crate of provisions from the hotel to the Boat Bar, a distance of about 100 yards. Boxes of ice, fine wines, glasses etcetera were all lugged by hand across the hot sand. We went out for the day and when we got back, we asked the staff how it had gone. "Not very well!" was the answer; apparently the passengers were all too decrepit to get from the ship to the boats, so nobody came to the party and all the stuff had to be hauled back to the hotel again. Lots of work and none of the anticipated big tips.

We hired a golf cart for the day, intending to visit

the island's cemetery, but within 50 feet of the hire company it broke down. They got it going again, but five minutes later we passed another one from the same company broken down and waiting for rescue. Another mile and there was yet another one in the same predicament. Inevitably, a few minutes later ours came to a grinding halt but as luck would have it, we were outside a bar on the edge of a particularly nice stretch of beach, so we had a drink and enjoyed the view while the barman phoned our people. In due course they came to fix it and I explained to the mechanic that we'd almost made it to the cemetery, but the cart had died before we got there. I don't think he got the joke, but then he was having a very bad day.

While he was working on it, I asked if there a horn on the cart, to which the answer was no. I asked him if there was a handbrake; there was, but on our machine it didn't work. In fact, the brakes didn't work at all, but – nothing ventured, nothing gained – we rigged up an emergency braking system in the form of a coconut that happened to be on the ground nearby. This we kept in the glove compartment and every time we parked, we'd shove the coconut under the tyre as a chock. I instructed Jilly that in the case of an emergency stop being needed she was to take the coconut, hop out, run to the front and pop the thing under the front tyre. Fortunately, the situation never arose, and we had a lovely day pottering around the island, pausing for pit stops every now and then. We went around the island clockwise, but we were starting to get dizzy so the next circuit was anti-clockwise.

That evening we were walking near our hotel when we spotted an interesting garden with ducks and goats and big tortoises behind a chain link fence. As we ambled by, I let out a loud burp and to our amusement the billy goat came rushing over to us, clearly impressed that a gringo could speak fluent goat. In the same garden there was a home-made hen house supported at the front by some breeze blocks, but it was the back support that caught our eye. On closer inspection we could see that it was a large bronze cannon. Interesting.

Most days on Big Corn were spent gently kayaking round the bay in the early morning sun, walking along the many different beaches, and swimming in the afternoons and ended with a spot of fishing before a shower and dinner. All terribly energetic. The people are polite, friendly, kind and helpful and the weather ranges from a minimum 70 degrees to highs of 90 with relatively low humidity, so it usually feels very pleasant indeed. There's a rain shower most days, usually in the evening and only lasting for half an hour or so. It's just enough to freshen things up – and the rain is always warm!

On one walk we came across a big house which was unusual in having three storeys and a flat roof;

most buildings are single storey and built on stilts to improve ventilation and stand up to the occasional hurricane. The house was situated at the tip of a headland on the windward side, so the sea crashed onto the rocky point and the flat roof took advantage of the dramatic views. The owner was a lovely eccentric lady with a huge hat and a great sense of humour. She'd opened up her house as a restaurant, and we enjoyed lunch there whilst she amused us with her infectious laugh.

I also went out with Elvis. He's changed a bit, as you'd expect. Now he's black, has a white beard and runs a fishing boat out of Little Corn. Uh huh huh...

We ate some wonderful food on Big Corn: prawns, lobster fish and steak at very reasonable prices, and extremely good. One day we bumped into an American couple we'd met on the Río San Juan, where Jilly swore I'd upset them at dinner over something I said when I'd had a few – but I found that hard to believe. Anyway, they had apparently forgiven me as they invited us to have dinner with them at a private house on the other side of the island, which was owned by a local widow who'd decided to make a bit of money by cooking for tourists on the occasional evening. We sat around a candle-lit table under the stars in her garden and enjoyed fresh lobster, wine and home-made coconut cookies for £20 per head.

In fact, we met loads of lovely Americans and

Canadians on our travels. I think you tend to meet a lot of kindred spirits when you go off the usual tourist trail, and we had such a laugh with most of them.

On our last night on the island we went to La Princess de la Isla for dinner. It's right on the beach in the middle of nowhere, and you can hear the sound of the sea meeting the shore. A delightful Italian couple run it; the wife, Constanta, is a chain smoker and reminded us of Sybil from Fawlty Towers. She has a hilarious laugh that starts from her boots and gradually gets higher and higher as she drinks more rum! They're such fun, and Mama makes the most marvellous food. It was the perfect setting for the final night of our Nicaraguan experience.

Part Three:

More Postcards from Mexico

Legal Wrangles, Broken Zips and Wrong Numbers

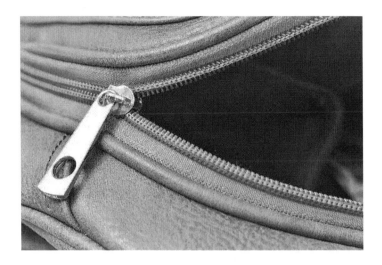

It was a close-run thing. Very close indeed.

We'd booked our flights to Mexico nearly a year ago and sold our house in July – or at least we thought we had, but the original buyers fizzled out after some weeks because her ex was still on the deeds of their house, and he wouldn't sign off. So fresh buyers were quickly found, but after six weeks they dropped out. As luck would have it, the first lot reappeared, having sorted out the ex, but we still hadn't exchanged contracts by Christmas, so everything stopped for over a week. When the lawyers went back to work it was looking as though we wouldn't complete until after we'd left the country, in which case our poor son would have to supervise the move. But then the lawyers decided they could exchange on the 7th January and complete on the 12th, the day before our flights!

Here is what happened next.

Jilly, who is so lithe and fit with all that yoga and Pilates plus plenty of gardening, ricked her back whilst clearing out a cupboard and was in extreme pain, which was to last for over a week. Rather than worry about rebuilding and making up the bed in our new home on moving day, we decided to book a room at a Travelodge for the night of the 12th from where we could walk to the station to catch the 5:23am train to Gatwick.

On the 11th my son and I moved two van loads of plants, flower pots, containers and garden statues to our new house. At a conservative estimate, I reckon this lot weighed about 2,000 tons.

Meanwhile, Jilly heard from our solicitor that the statutory declaration I'd had to get notarised a couple of weeks earlier needed to be signed by me. I'd queried this at the time with the notary, but she'd assured me that it was only her that needed to sign, not me, due to a 'weird legal anomaly'. So it meant I had to go back the next day – moving day – to sign this wretched form.

I checked our paperwork and discovered to my dismay that the booking I'd made at the Travelodge was actually for the 7th, not the 12th as intended, and it was too late to change it. I just had to grin and bear it and book the room again, at a cost of another £60. Naughty words were muttered ... well, bellowed, actually.

Come the day of the move and Jilly, still in great pain, had finished packing our holiday stuff and was zipping up the second case when the zip broke. Oh joy!

I drove off to get the form signed, only to find that the solicitor couldn't find it. Three secretaries searched high and low for half an hour before it turned up. Then I raced to the other end of the High Street to the naughty notary, sat and fumed until she got off the phone and came down to apologise, signed the damned thing and rushed back to our solicitor – who then wanted to chat about the completion mechanics and Mexico.

On the way back to the car park I popped into a charity shop and managed to find two decent suitcases. I bought them both and drove home, only to find that our son and daughter-in-law had kindly loaned us one of their cases and Jilly had just finished re-packing it! Jilly was too exhausted and in too much pain to face having to re-pack yet again and I wouldn't have even liked to attempt it.

Whilst I was out and the removal van was being packed a chap who rode his bike past our cottage every working day on his way to work and back suddenly accosted Jilly and demanded to know why she hadn't told him the place was for sale as he would have loved to have bought it!

The removal men were hard at work; they had cleared the office of the filing cabinet and desk, so it only remained for me to dismantle the computer spaghetti. Just as I started pulling out the plugs Jilly remembered that we hadn't checked in online for our flights, so I stuffed the plugs back in and somehow managed to get the laptop working again, but when I got on the BA website there was no mention of Jilly, only me! Oh God, I thought, don't tell me it's only me going to Mexico. In a panic I phoned them and was passed from one pressed button to another until I finally got through to an Indian with a very strong accent, to whom I tried to explain our predicament. To my huge relief, I hadn't forgotten to book Jilly in and the problem was of BA's making, not mine. She was duly checked in, but by this time the printer had been packed and the van had left, so I couldn't print the confirmations. It was left that we'd have to sort it out at Gatwick – something else to worry about!

By this time the purchasers' removal men had arrived and wanted to start unloading, but we still hadn't finished packing last minute stuff. Just then the cavalry arrived in the form of our sons, so they helped shift the last of the stuff whilst I tried to keep the incoming removal men at bay. Then we got a call from the solicitor to say completion had gone through, our cottage was now sold, and we had to let the new owners start moving into the place we'd called home for 41 years. A few tears were shed.

They say that moving home is one of the most stressful things in life, but that was just ridiculous!

We got everything into the new place and our son took us to the hotel, where we had a quiet dinner and tried to unwind before hitting the sack in readiness for a 4am alarm. Next morning, I had a quick shower during which I inadvertently flooded the bathroom and had to mop up as best I could with the remaining towels.

Finally, things got better. Our trains were uneventful – except that I'd overheard a blind chap in the seat behind telling the ticket collector he wanted to get off at Redhill, but when we got there I realised he was asleep. I prodded him awake and told him we were at Redhill and he was half out of his seat before I realised that we were, in fact, at Reigate and I'd read the wrong sign, so he had to sit down again. I like to help people.

At Gatwick it was as though we were VIPs. We steamed through check in and security like a dose of salts, leaving us time for breakfast, a bit of shopping and the three-mile hike along Gatwick's interminable corridors to our terminal, where we were waved straight onto the plane. It left pretty much on time and the flight was uneventful, but we knew we had hideous Cancun airport to come. Last time it was like a zoo, with umpteen planes landing at the same time and thousands of tired and grumpy passengers being forced to wait for over two hours to get through the immigration formalities. Guess what? This time it was like a different airport, and as at Gatwick we were through quickly and efficiently.

I knew it was too good to last! As we stepped out of the airport doors, we were met by the usual hordes of Mexicans carrying boards with the names of expected visitors but, unusually, it was dark and pouring with rain, driven in by very strong winds. We eventually found the ride we'd booked and off we set in his van, but halfway to our resort the driver's boss phoned to say that the credit card number I'd given him when we booked was not working, and would I please check that he'd got the right numbers? So I had to try and read the shiny numbers on my battered credit card in the dark in a van that was bouncing around after 20 hours travel and the most stressful 48 hours the world has ever known. I remained patient and calm (liar!) and did my best but it still didn't work so we tried another card and solved that particular problem.

The next challenge, as though we needed any more, was to find the place we'd booked. The address we'd been given was very vague but there was a phone number for the owner, and our instructions were to phone when we got to Puerto Morelos and she would give our driver precise directions and meet us there. Well, of course our driver couldn't get through to the number we'd been given. He kept trying but it was no good. Fortunately, I had a pretty good idea where the apartment was, having stayed in the same town before, so we got as close as I could tell him and then the driver parked and got out to ask around in the pouring rain. Amazingly, the owner was already there and waiting for us! She let us in, showed us round, offered us a drink and we finally crashed out, relieved and thankful that all the stress was behind us and we could concentrate on six whole weeks of our next adventure.

Barracudas, Gringo Traps
and Missing Colours

The rain was still falling when we awoke next morning, but after 20 cups of tea it stopped and we ventured out to explore. The apartment was less than a minute's walk from the lovely beach and a beach bar with sun loungers under brollies, which were free if you bought a drink, so this was a good start. We were also only a quiet stroll four blocks from the centre of town, which had restaurants, bars and shops. All in all, it was a great location. When we stayed at Puerto Morelos last year we were in a cabin about an hour's walk from town, so it was good to be so central this time.

We walked to the nearest restaurant for breakfast and were soon chatting to an American on the next table. "What do you guys think about Jeremy Corbyn?" he asked. Always discreet, I told him that Corbyn would soon be kicked out as he was too left wing, which turned out to be the wrong answer as our new friend turned out to be even more of a leftie. Hush my mouth!

We had a nice wander around town, bought some provisions, then walked back to our place for some lunch on the little patio area. The rest of the day was spent just slobbing around and recovering from the madness of the previous few days.

The next day was hot and sunny, so after a walk along the beach and a bit more shopping we made our way to the beach bar for an afternoon siesta, only to discover it was Happy Hour, so we – okay, I – was forced to sample a couple of margaritas whilst Jilly enjoyed something more in line with dry January. It was very relaxing.

That evening, when most of the swimmers had gone, I tried a bit of fishing from the beach. I caught a lovely little barracuda on a spinner; I put him back, like a good boy, but next day at dawn his big brother paid me a visit and he wasn't so lucky. We cooked him for lunch and very nice he was, too.

We do like this little seaside town. It's only about half an hour's drive from Cancun airport and is so sleepy and welcoming, with its quiet streets and gentle, friendly people. Just right for unwinding for a few days after a long flight.

We were pleased with our apartment. It had a breakfast bar, kitchen, decent bathroom, big bedroom and patio doors out to a yard enclosed by high walls on top of which iguanas sunned themselves – and all for £30 a night. However, a number of problems cropped up to entertain us. The gas ran out, which meant no cooking or hot water, the front door lock broke and the patio door was sticking. We tried to phone the owner but couldn't get through, so we sent a text and an email. I fixed the patio door with a candle rubbed on the tracking, and when the owner got the text she put the rest right. We even gave her half the barracuda as it was too big for us.

The days whipped by and, much refreshed, we packed up and left Puerto on a bus for a five-hour drive to La Laguna de Siete Colores, or 'The Lake of Seven Colours', at a town called Bacalar some 200 miles south. It was a pleasant easy journey apart from the usual icy air conditioning, but we had warm clothes handy, so it wasn't a problem. Jilly's back was still tender, but she had a heated stick-on patch and a comfortable seat. Our journey took us past miles of green forest and the odd sleepy-looking Mexican village on superb roads, often dead straight for great distances.

Our next home in Bacalar turned out to be right on the main square and again was self-contained. To one side of the tree-lined square was an 18th century Spanish fort, initially built to protect the town from pirates but subsequently seeing action when the Mayans rose up against the ruling Spanish in the 19th century. Down below was the lake, with lovely shades of blue and indigo – but we never counted seven colours. Sadly, they didn't give refunds.

We enjoyed some long walks by the lake and around the sleepy town. Although we were staying on the square there was very little traffic; the most noise came from the birds, who set up an almighty row at dawn and dusk. There was a good, cheap restaurant almost next door where we enjoyed steak dinners with wine and water for £12 for the two of us. Even cheaper was a little fast food cart with a thatched roof (!) which sold quesadillas with a vast range of fillings. Jilly liked the avocado whilst I preferred pork. We enjoyed watching the cooking process, overseen by Mama whilst her daughter kneaded the dough and flattened it in a lever-operated machine. All this entertainment, including Spanish lessons, came to about £1.10 for a tasty lunch for two. Of course, we had to round it off at the gelato shop around the corner where they had loads of flavours – including red wine!

One thing we noticed about Bacalar was the number of gringo traps. My theory is that as Mexicans struggle to reach any height over 5' there is no reason to position shop blinds and other projections at anything over 5'8". That's all fine until a 6' gringo, with hat pulled low to keep the sun out of his eyes, smacks into the blind, head first. Time after time. Finally wising up, I started looking up as I walked, only to risk tripping on holes in the pavements, sleeping dogs and steel rods sticking out of the ground that once served to anchor long-lost telegraph poles. Only yesterday I smashed my head into a concrete arch over a flight of stairs. I doubt if the arch was more than 5'6" high. The concussion is gradually wearing off.

We wanted to go on a boat trip around the lake, but although there were plenty of blokes trying to sell you a cruise, they all relied on getting at least four people in order to make it economically viable. If they worked together from a central booking office this would be fine, but they don't; they all work independently so if you say you want to go you have to wait for two more punters to turn up. There were precious few tourists around and we kept getting fed up with waiting and wandered off elsewhere. To cut a long story short, we persevered and did eventually get our boat ride – and very nice it was, too.

Alaskan Buses, Mayan Temples and Rubber Ducks

Using Jilly's poorly back as a thin excuse, we booked Fernando and his taxi to take us from Bacalar to our next home in the small town of Xpujil, which sounds like the sort of noise you might make after too many drinks followed by a hot curry. It's pronounced Shpookill in English, or something similar.

Anyway, Fernando drove along the dead straight Mexican highway at a steady 110kph, pausing only to trundle over the many sleeping policemen, which they call topes, and also for the occasional army check points, where fierce-looking soldiers toting serious guns were apparently on the lookout for illegal immigrants from other Central American countries. They just waved us on, fortunately.

The roads continued in their dead straight, monotonous fashion past acres of sugar cane plantations and fields of pineapples, but mostly flat jungle and scrubland. It was warm, and pretty soon my head was nodding. It was at this point that Fernando decided to have a chat, but there was no gentle introduction. It was, in fact, like a machine gun going off. Fernando had two modes: complete silence for twenty minutes, then 1000-decibel rapid fire Spanish. Of course, I nearly s--t myself, which Fernando found highly amusing. This was repeated several times during the 90-minute journey and I found no further need for roughage for the rest of the day.

We duly arrived at the Hotel Calakmul in Xpujil, which was to be our base for the next four nights. The town is on a crossroads in the middle of nowhere, but right in the middle of something like 40 ancient Mayan sites, the most important being (surprise surprise) Calakmul. In other words, it's a perfect jumping-off point for ruins-bashing.

The hotel was clearly in the middle of a big clean up. A mop and bucket stood in the posh reception area, and a brush and pan were leaning against the restaurant counter. There was nobody in the reception area, but we waited around for a while, noticing that the hardwood counter top was thick with dust. Eventually, we found a lady in the restaurant area who checked the register and denied all knowledge of a Robinson booking. I looked over her shoulder and immediately spotted 'Andrew Robinson' written in for the four days we'd booked. "Ah, si," she said, when I pointed it out. But our room was not yet ready as they were cleaning that, too. So we had lunch there and then picked up the room key.

That afternoon we went to relax by the pool but only minutes after we arrived a very loud generator burst into life, accompanied by a dreadful pong. Looking behind us, we realised they were emptying the septic tank. Lovely. Ten minutes later the noise and the pong stopped as they finished and the lorry drove off, so we settled back to enjoy the peace, only to have it all start up again 20 minutes later as they came back for part two. And then part three! Enough! We went for a walk around town instead.

During the time we were there the mop and bucket and the broom never moved and the only change to the dusty reception desk was that I daringly wrote 'limpio' (clean) in the dust. But the room was fine, the pool area was pretty and most welcome after a hot morning traipsing around ruins and there were hummingbirds to be seen flitting about the well-planted grounds. For £21 a night we didn't feel too badly done by.

That night at dinner we met our first ever Alaskan, who confessed that many of his fellow countrymen headed south just to get away from the almost perpetual darkness at this time of the year. His name, he said, was Stretch – and at 6'8" with a beard and ponytail I wasn't going to contradict him. He had a campervan and spent winters exploring warmer climes; next morning he was off to Guatemala, presumably in his stretch limo.

We splurged on an organised tour the next day to the lost city of Calakmul, buried deep in the jungle and very difficult to get to without either a taxi or a tour. We were due to be picked up from our hotel at 7:30 but no one had turned up by 7:40 and I was getting angry. We'd travelled over 5,000 miles and managed to be in the right place at the right time, but their office was only 500 yards down the road and they were late. I asked the hotel gardener if he could phone the tour people for us, but as he opened his mobile, I saw that it was 6:40, not 7:40. How could this be? Answer: our drive yesterday had taken us into a different state where they were an hour ahead, but I hadn't twigged and we were basically an hour early as a result. I decided to let them off in view of the circumstances.

Our guide drove us for some two hours along a very narrow road hemmed in on both sides by wall-to-wall trees, during which we spotted oscillated turkeys and a couple of peccaries. Then followed a very atmospheric walking tour with a bit of pyramid climbing and lots of interesting fauna and flora. And guess what? Our fellow passenger turned out to be Alaskan as well. Two in two days – a bit like waiting for a bus! He was the same age as me and he came out with a lovely one-liner: "I may be old but I'm slow!"

We were intrigued by the number of what we referred to as 'rubber ducks' in Xpujil. These were huge American trucks with shiny chrome vertical exhaust pipes, often hauling two monster trailers and looking as brightly lit up as a Christmas tree at night. Xpujil turned out to be an important stopping point for them on their east/west journeys, and for us we were reminded of films like *Smokey and the Bandit* and the days of CB radio: "Rubber Duck, Rubber Duck, c'mon Rubber Duck, this here's a convoy!" Whatever all that meant.

We found a great little outdoor place for lunch. They only served pulled pork with either tacos or nachos. Not being too sure what either meant we chose tacos, as Jilly thought nachos were somehow like Doritos, and she's not fond of them. The bloke cooked the pork and chopped it up with a huge knife while the lady cooked the flatbread and they served up the resulting treat with a slice of lemon and a choice of hot salsa or very hot salsa. With a couple of beers and some camomile tea (served ice cold and fizzy!), it came to about £2 and was so good we went back the following day.

There were two Mayan sites about six miles away and close together, so we negotiated a price with a taxi driver to take us to the first site, wait an hour or so for us to amble round, then take us to the second site and wait for another hour before taking us back to the hotel. All this for £12. As well as the Mayan stuff, we also spotted a fox (did you know the Spanish for fox is Zorro?) and a squirrel, both a lot smaller than our British ones.

On our last evening we went out for dinner at our favourite restaurant and a gringo appeared at the next table. Taking a wild guess, I said: "Are you from Alaska?" to which he was visibly startled. "How the hell did you know?" he said. I don't know who was the more amazed – him or us.

Bulldog, Grunts
and The House of Dreams

We left Xpujil for the two-hour drive to Mahahual on the coast, stopping at a beach bar for a light lunch of guacamole and a couple of drinks before hiring a taxi to take us first to buy some provisions and then for the 30-mile ride to the most southerly town on the Mexican Caribbean coast, Xcalak. The road was dead straight, jungle trying to crowd in on both sides, and we didn't meet a single vehicle for the entire journey.

Xcalak is the last stop before Belize and is part of a national park so we'd been told to stop off at the park office to buy bracelets authorising us to swim, snorkel, kayak and basically live within the park. But guess what? It was siesta time – so we hung about for ten minutes until 4pm when the sign said they'd open again. By quarter past they were still snoozing so, rather than keep the taxi driver waiting, we set off on the final leg of that day's journey, which was six miles on a dirt track running north along the coast.

Finally, we arrived at our destination, a beach house perched right on the sea. Depending on the time of day and the clouds, the colours are constantly changing and about half a mile out the full force of the open sea smashes onto the Mesoamerican reef with a dull, continuous roar. The white breakers there are clearly visible, but within the reef the sea is protected and calm, with many coral heads showing as dark spots amongst the indigos and greens.

Behind us was the dense jungle and lagoons connected to the huge bay of Chetumal; the dirt track runs for miles beyond, which makes for super long walks through dappled shade if the tide is too high for beach walks.

Our new home was a self-contained apartment with en suite and constant hot water. We stayed here for a very happy week and it was extremely relaxing. Jilly's back was nearly fixed and she was doing Pilates again whilst I went fishing. They had kayaks for the free use of guests, and every afternoon I set off in the single seater with my rod, paddled out and dropped anchor to catch beautifully coloured fish with the not so beautiful but very descriptive name of grunts. It took me a week to work out how best to catch these fish, but I think I finally got the knack. A whole week to outwit a fish? Doesn't say much for my IQ, does it?

The owners were Americans, John and Sue. He was very macho and extremely opinionated. Jilly thought he was possessive of Sue and initially I found him domineering. However, Jilly noticed he was always tearing about the property trying to fix problems with the generator or the motorbike or whatever and cursing as he did so, only to find that as often as not there was no problem at all; he reminded her of a character in the TV series *Frasier* called Bulldog. Bulldog is an ex-jock sports reporter at a US radio station who is always saying things like "This stinks! Someone's stolen my pen," only to find it in his other pocket seconds later and say: "Oh, that's okay then." And so it was that John became Bulldog in our minds.

The beach walks were most pleasant once you get used to the fact that it's largely a wild coast with no one to pick up the wind- and tide-blown flotsam once you get past the residences, which are few and far between. On the tidewrack was a jumble of natural debris: seaweed, coconuts and shells – most notably big conch shells – intermingled with manmade plastics like bottles, fishing detritus in the form of nets and ropes, polystyrene buoys and the inevitable flip flops. But we could walk for about a mile in each direction and it was so pleasant to do so after breakfast.

Ah, breakfast! Every morning Jilly made up a delectable assortment of diced tropical fruit smothered in local yoghurt, followed by some slimming slices of cake and coffee or tea. The type of fruit depended on what the food truck brought. It visited just about every day and you never knew what delights it would offer. The first thing you knew of its presence was a brief burst of car alarm, and we all rushed to the track clutching purses and wallets. The truck driver hopped out holding his calculator whilst his mate sat in the open back behind a set of scales, surrounded by a sea of fruit and veg, meat and bread, all as fresh as you could wish for. Typically, we bought the best tomatoes you've ever tasted, bananas, peaches, apples, the sweetest, most succulent pineapples in the world, ripe avocados, melon, really sweet oranges, ham, bread, tortillas etcetera etcetera, all for absurdly little money. The chap in the back seemed to know exactly how much you needed and the calculator man totted it up.

But some days there was real excitement! One day the truck specialised only in cake. Rich, divine homemade cake with cinnamon and raisins and all sorts of naughty ingredients. Jilly bought one the size of a wedding cake that kept us happy for days, and she also bought me a delightful treat in the form of a frozen individual-sized homemade cheesecake set on a base of raw grated coconut from the tree in Mama's garden. Wow!

Another day the truck contained only huge, freshly caught prawns. I bought six for bait and made the mistake of telling the lady what they were for. She nearly wept and said it was such a waste. One day a chap came by with a one-dish menu for takeaway that his missus cooked – it was a bit like spring rolls but crammed with pulled pork and veg, and cost about three pence.

The only other guests were a Canadian couple in their sixties, Ted and Helen. Ted was a mad keen fly fisherman and very sociable, but for the first three days we never saw Helen other than a shadowy figure in a floaty dress on their upstairs balcony. We began to think she was a bit like the invisible Margaret in the *Little Britain* series, where the shopkeeper yells upstairs "Margaret, Margaret!" and nods reassuringly to the waiting customer. On our fourth day there, Bulldog had a bonfire on the beach to which we were invited, and Helen showed up. She was very pleasant but a tad antisocial. Bulldog, of course, was holding court with his extreme views on just about every subject, which caused us some amusement. Most of the time we were distracted by shooting stars, fireflies and ten million stars; this part of the coast has zero light pollution.

Walking north along the track we couldn't believe the sheer number and variety of butterflies – it's almost as though it's snowing butterflies in places. They're obviously attracted to the flowering shrubs, and of course various birds are in turn attracted to the butterflies and the flowers, so we caught glimpses of hummingbirds and orioles (no, not the biscuits), very fancy with their yellow and orange livery. We heard many more birds but by and large they were a bit on the furtive side. Every night a little owl set up a strange chorus, but we never saw him. Over the sea there were razorbills, frigate birds trying to rob them whenever they caught anything, and squadrons of pelicans crash-diving into the drink. Storks, ibis and herons stood like statues in the shallows.

This is something of an eco-friendly place, with solar heating (most of the time) and a compost bin for biodegradable rubbish. Guarding this bin were a couple of large iguanas who greatly appreciated the little veggie treats their human slaves brought them. The 'eco' bit involves not using electricity at night, but we were provided with lots of candles, which meant Jilly cooked at night on the gas hob via candlelight and headlamp torch. Had we been a tad younger it might even have been romantic!

For some reason I didn't snorkel until our last day, which was a shame as the water was incredibly warm. There was no shock to the system when taking the plunge, and lots of colourful fish and corals to see. When I'd had enough, I was swimming back to the beach when I came face to face with a huge barracuda, who stared straight at me as though deciding whether to take a chunk out of me or not. Fortunately, he casually finned off into the deep. Where the hell was he when I was fishing?

On our last day, Ted, the Canadian, kindly volunteered to take us into Xcalak to grab a taxi to our next home. Next thing we knew, he was driving in the opposite direction, along the dead straight main road back to Mahahual. "Where are you going, Ted?" we asked him, to which he replied that he knew we were heading back to Mahahual and as it was a bit too windy to fish he thought he'd just drive us the 30 miles there. How very kind. We bought him a box of his favourite cigars when we arrived and off he went back to Xcalak. A truly nice man.

In Mahahual we stopped for lunch, bought a few provisions and then took a taxi the 7km ride to Kohunbeach Cabanas, which is at the other end of the dirt track we'd left that same morning.

Windsor Soup, Boiled Eggs and Leaks

We arrived at Kohunbeach Cabanas to be met by an elderly and thoroughly lovely American named Janet, who runs the place with her equally lovely chap, Guillermo, or Memo to his friends.

Our home this time was one of only three cabins, each with a hexagonal base some 20 feet across, within which was a big double bed, wardrobe, settee and lots of insect-screened windows facing the sea. Above this spacious room was a lofty thatched roof and at the rear was a well-equipped en suite. A covered patio area at the front took advantage of the views, with the sea only 20 yards away. The grounds were beautifully planted with palms and flowering shrubs, and there were at least six dogs to welcome us and bark at strangers.

We asked Janet if it was okay to use our travel kettle and were somewhat put out when she said absolutely not. Disaster, darling! But when we explained how important it was for Jilly to be drip fed tea 24/7, she immediately volunteered to provide thermos flasks full of hot water whenever we required, so problem solved, sort of.

However, there was still trouble at t' mill as the weather had taken a turn for the worse. Occasionally at this time of the year the Gulf of Mexico gets what they call 'Norte' – in other words, northerly winds – and with the eastern coast of the USA having had one of the worst winter storms for many years, the ripples had spread this far south. Not that we got 25" of snow – the temperature was still in the 70s – but the wind was decidedly cool and, more to the point, there was quite a lot of rain. And then there was the sea. Here it was no longer clear and blue. What we had was brown Windsor soup, full of torn up weed, and some pretty hefty breakers which were visibly eating their way up the beach, to the point that the roots of the seafront palm trees were almost totally exposed. That night the noise of the breakers was so loud and violent that it felt as though we'd be swept away at any moment, and we were relieved when we were still alive and dry at daybreak.

But the next day was not much better. The weather was still pants, and the promised included breakfast took ages to appear on a communal table under a palapa, but we had no clue as to which bit was ours and which was for the other guests. We sort of worked it out by the number of boiled eggs, assuming there was one egg for each guest. On that basis we reckoned that we constituted 50% of the guests so we grabbed half – fresh cakes, fruit, and coffee and hot water in flasks.

There was Wi-Fi, but it was patchy to say the least. It was constantly dropping off, and to re-start it, Jilly had to go to a certain post by the track and log on from there. Frequently!

By this time, we'd pretty much decided that this place was not for us, so we hitched a ride with Memo into Mahahual where we found the same drizzly weather but calm, clear seas and a multitude of bars, restaurants, hotels and shops. We spent some time there walking into hotels and checking on prices and facilities. Finally, we decided on Hotel Mexico Lindo, one block in from the prom but modern and clean, with en suite airconditioned rooms surrounding a beautifully planted atrium for £24 a night. Bear in mind the Travelodge in Swindon wanted to charge us £80 a night in January! We paid for five nights and took a taxi back to Kohunbeach.

As soon as we got back, we told Janet we'd

decided to cut short our stay with her but assured her we were quite prepared to pay for the days we'd booked. Janet, to her credit, wouldn't hear of it and insisted that we only pay for the days we stayed there. We didn't argue too hard.

That evening we walked about half a mile down the track to the nearest restaurant, which was run by a charming Dutchman called Albert who served great food and wine at very reasonable prices. There just happened to be a live group playing that night, three old boys from the Midwest of America who played lots of easy listening US country music, most of which we'd never heard before. The restaurant rapidly filled with Americans who all seemed to know each other and talked at huge volume throughout the performance.

We spent two more nights at Janet's and enjoyed some pleasant walks. We tried to launch the kayak on a calmer day but there was still too much wind, so we had to give up on that. However, I did splash out on a morning fishing trip which resulted in one small barracuda and about 20 smaller fish using cut bait, and three big fish hooked briefly – each one lost, to my great annoyance.

We went back to Albert's restaurant for another great meal and decided to buy Janet a voucher for dinner with wine for two as we still felt guilty. That last night the rain came down and the sea was even noisier, so we didn't get much sleep. To make matters worse, our thatched roof developed some leaks, so we had to use our ice box to collect the drips, and then something strange happened to the lights meaning some sort of strobe flashed every few seconds all night!

Janet kept to her word and only charged us for the nights we stayed, even including a discount, and Memo drove us into Mahahual to our 'posh' new home at Mexico Lindo, where we didn't have to stand on one leg in the rain to get Wi-Fi. Things were looking up – and so was the weather.

(Note: Did you spot the giant lizard overlooking our hotel? Before you go rushing off to Google which hotel it is, I'd better admit that our son-in-law Photoshopped it in for a bit of fun!)

Wheelbarrows, Hammocks and Thieving Pelicans

The weather on our first day in Mahahual was still cool and drizzly, but we were happy enough to walk along the pedestrian-only paved promenade, known as the Malecon, until we got to the dock where a few posh cruisers were moored. There was also a glass-bottomed catamaran to view the underwater scene on the coral reef if you didn't fancy snorkelling, and a couple of Customs boats. A few locals were fishing, some choosing to drop their hand lines down drainpipe-sized holes in the dock, presumably for drainage. It looked very like fishing through the ice, but they were catching little fish.

In due course we adjourned to a nearby restaurant on the beach to sample a margarita or two. Or was it three? The tide was right out and the wading birds stood in very little water. I said to Jilly, "Those birds are going to run out of money soon," so perhaps it was three margaritas after all...

Next morning was brighter and after a bit of fishing off the dock we had a leisurely lunch at the nearby beach restaurant. The sun came out and the day became hot, so we just relaxed on their sun loungers and watched the water. After the poor weather it was a bit like the song *Hello Muddah Hello Fadduh* – "Guys are swimming, guys are sailing" etc. Kayaks, stand-up paddle boards, banana boat rides, snorkelling, people fly fishing as they waded through the shallow, protected lagoon... And beautiful colours to the sea. It would be very easy to let the day drift by – which we did, cheerfully.

That evening we tried a 'hole in the wall' cafe run by some Uruguayan ladies who cooked mysterious and very tasty food before your very eyes for not much money. From our table on the pavement we watched the money changer next door shut up shop but then carry on trading from his balcony above the kiosk. People rang a bell and he lowered a screw top jar on the end of a string. Customers would put their dollars in the jar and he would haul it up, count it, put the corresponding amount in pesos in the jar and lower it back down. Ingenious and secure.

The place where we'd bought the cigars for Ted, the Canadian, was run by a knowledgeable and charming bearded Mexican who never got off his stool; he directed his staff to get any article we wanted, and initially I thought he was perhaps disabled and unable to walk. His shop doubled as the ticket office for buses out of Mahahual. One evening we decided to eat out at a restaurant called Fernando's 100% Agave, which had been recommended. Imagine our surprise when Fernando – an immensely tall man wearing a Panama hat – turned out to be the very same chap who also sold the cigars and bus tickets. So much for my theory!

We splashed out on another fishing boat trip next day, in a sea that looked like royal blue Swan ink. The captain caught a big barracuda, maybe 20lbs, and I had the tail bitten off my plastic lure which rendered it useless. After a couple of hours trolling with no further action, we anchored in deep water and tried using chunks of sardine. We caught a few small ones and then I hooked into something very big and strong. Jilly thought my rod was going to snap, but after two minutes of tug of war the fish cheated and bit through the line. I wasn't doing too well with these Mexican whoppers – so far...

That afternoon, two huge cruise ships docked and disgorged thousands of mostly American tourists who were taxied from the port some two miles away into Mahahual. The little town was transformed! Lots of Mexicans appeared, putting up stalls to sell souvenirs, or setting up massage parlours on the beach. A chap with a monkey on a lead magically appeared for 'photo opportunities', shops put out signs advertising Viagra and so on. It made for brilliant people watching for us, but then we retreated to our favourite restaurant; it was too far for most of the cruise ship passengers to walk so we had peace.

However, two elderly Americans did turn up and, after a few drinks, decided to take a kayak out. It was a single seater, which they clearly didn't realise. She got in facing the wrong way. Then he got in behind her, also facing the wrong way. At this time the kayak was still resting on the sand, but as soon as he pushed it into deeper water it capsized, of course – as did we, with suppressed laughter! They were only in shallow water, so no harm done. He then went back to the bar to complain and they gently explained to him that it was a single seater and also that it worked better with the pointy end at the front. So back he went to the kayak, clambered in and set off in a huff, leaving his wife standing there with her paddle but no boat. Where do they get 'em?

It soon became too hot for me in the sun, so I relocated to a hammock strung between two branches of an ancient mangrove tree, swaying gently over crystal clear, lukewarm water with lots of little fish swimming below. Lunch had been more than good: Jilly had a heaped plate of ceviche and I had a mountain of shrimp tacos, three bottles of beer, tea for Jilly, all served at a table set in the shallows of a blue lagoon with our feet in the warm water and the sun hot on our backs. The cost of all this? £7 each. And Jilly thought that was a bit pricey! It was a pleasant life indeed.

One evening we enjoyed the sunset from the dock, but then Jilly left to go back and shower while I decided to fish on for a bit longer. The pelicans kept trying to nick my bait, and then they were after the fish I was catching whilst I was still reeling it in. By this time, I was alone on the dock and surrounded by the pesky birds, both on land and sea. When I caught the next fish, I managed to steer it past the water-borne pelicans but then the land lubbers actually chased me round as I was trying to unhook it! Quite fearless, they were, but I was not, so I decided discretion was the better part of valour and gave it up as a bad job.

We had some great meals in Mahahual – shrimp fajitas, ceviche etc. – and felt very safe there. But all too soon it was time to move on yet again. While Jilly was packing, I went for a walk. About a mile out of town I came across an elderly couple, each pushing an ancient, squeaking wheelbarrow laden with coconuts. They were on their way to town to sell them to the fresh coconut milk vendors, but they were clearly struggling, so I grabbed the lady's barrow and we walked together trying to converse in Spanish. After a while we noticed that her old man was lagging behind, and she explained he'd got a bad leg, so I pushed his for a while, too. Well, I couldn't let Jilly do all the work!

Ruinous Swimming, Noisy Blighters and the Mexican Banksie

We enjoyed our two-and-a-half-hour bus ride to Tulum. All the buses we've been on have been excellent. Punctual, lots of leg room, comfortable seats, often with TV, and as the main roads are so very good and straight the ride is smooth even at a top speed limit of 100kph. The only problem is when the driver is in the sun: he turns the aircon up (or should that be down?) to 30 below so he is comfortable whilst the passengers freeze. Nowadays we always come prepared with long trousers, fleeces and blankets (yes, really!).

On arrival in Tulum we collected our cases and walked out of the bus station, only realising afterwards that we'd completely ignored all the signs forbidding passengers from exiting via the bus access – we should have gone out of the front entrance. But hey, you're only young once and life's for living, innit?

Our next home was still being cleaned in readiness for us to wreck it, so we found a hippy hostel right opposite the bus station where they were still serving breakfast (at 12:30?) and we pigged ourselves on pancakes and maple syrup.

When we were able to access our apartment, we discovered it was far larger than we'd gathered from the Airbnb website. Only one block away from the main drag, it was set behind a high steel gate opening into a lovely walled garden. The apartment itself was 30' x 14' with a spacious en suite, kitchen (including purified water), and hardwood wooden shutters with flyscreens behind. We were well pleased.

Tulum is noted for its Mayan ruins, dramatically set on a cliff top overlooking a white sand beach and gorgeous coloured sea. We'd been there before, and Jilly had long held an ambition to swim in the sea below the ruins, so this was our main objective. The town itself is set about two miles from the ruins, and we'd never been there. We were amazed to discover how big it was, with lots of shops, bars and restaurants.

We greatly enjoyed walking around to get our bearings, and of course we had to have the odd tea break – especially at Happy Hour, which appears to be any time the particular bar needs more customers. I do approve of the Mexicans' grasp of business sense and do everything in my power to help them.

Next day we took a taxi to the ruins and made our way to the rickety rackety wooden staircase down the cliff to the beach. People of every nationality were going up or down, plus of course the inevitable Japanese tourists, complete with all-weather protection including gloves and brollies, standing halfway down taking pictures so nobody could move in either direction.

We took it in turns to go into the water whilst the other one guarded our 'valuables' and took photos. The sea this day was rough, and we were bashed by the surging waves, but they were warm and we were happy to be there. Then we stood on the soft sand and let the sun dry us out before doing the 'towel round the waist' changing routine so beloved of day trippers at the seaside all over the world. Have you ever noticed that, as you try to put the second leg into your pants, your big toe always gets snagged and you end up hopping around, desperately hoping you don't fall over whilst trying to hang onto the towel that keeps threatening to fall off? We noticed that some Russian blokes didn't bother with all that modesty nonsense and just stripped off, regardless.

Iguanas of every size emerged from the cliff behind us, some chasing each other, some nodding heads as a warning or an amorous signal, others coming right onto the beach and frightening the bejesus out of dozing tourists who suddenly realised there was a large, prehistoric dragon right next to them. Oh, how we enjoyed people watching.

Eventually, we made our way back through the ruins to the exit and then onto Tulum's public beach, which is considered to be one of the finest in Mexico: miles of firm, white sand backed by dunes and fronted by the lovely blue Caribbean. There we found a watering hole and had a good lunch before walking a mile or so along the beach, just enjoying the hot sun and the sound of the surf. How lucky we were.

We took a taxi home and, after hot showers, found an excellent family-owned Italian/Mexican restaurant, with him fishing and her cooking. A good combination of talents and a very tasty end product.

We have observed that Mexicans have a very different concept of noise to the Brits. That night being a Friday night was a good illustration of this. Bear in mind we were a block away from the main road, and in this country, there are always cockerels crowing at all times, and dogs barking too. Various street vendors prowled around until about midnight, each one with a loudspeaker playing their various jingles at ten billion decibels – apart from the bread man, who pedalled around on a trike squeezing his old-fashioned bicycle horn. But at about 3am someone nearby started sweeping. It was quite soothing, as it happens, but somewhat odd at that time of the morning. Shortly after, a car or truck pulled up outside; it had a clunky diesel engine that the owner left running. Naturally they had no option but to shout above the engine noise to make themselves heard. What else could they do? This went on for at least ten minutes before they drove off, and then all was peaceful apart from the thumping bass of the faraway nightclub for the hard of hearing. Interspersed with all this was the occasional heavy lorry thundering past on this otherwise quiet residential street – just in case you needed any help in staying awake. Oh, and there was a marching band as well, but you could hardly hear them for the other noisy buggers.

Next day we decided to explore the back streets, where the tourists don't normally go. We found all sorts of obscure churches, little shops and tiny cafes, as well as posh houses and tin shacks. Everyone we met had a smile and a polite greeting for us – except some of the dogs. Most places have a dog or two in their garden and if you don't look at them, they're happy to snooze away the day, but if you make eye contact, they seem to take it as a threat or a challenge and switch to full guard dog mode, running at you and barking furiously. Thankfully, the really vicious ones are either on a rope or behind a fence, and the others keep their distance so long as you keep moving away from them.

Right at the start of this trek I'd brought with me some clip-on Polaroid sunglasses to help when it was really bright, but I'd not only dropped them in a taxi but inadvertently trodden on them as well. They had to be chucked and we'd been nowhere big enough to buy replacements ever since. However, on the free map of Tulum we'd spotted an optician's, so we navigated our way to his shop only to find it was siesta time and he wouldn't be open again until 4pm. We wandered around for another half hour and got back at four, but there was no sign of life, so we did some more walking, none of it a chore and all of it interesting. Eventually we got back to the shop and alleluia, he was not only open, but he had 'butterflies' for sale at a price we could afford. However, they were too big. No problem: he took out his scissors and cut them to size for no extra money. Now I could throw away that white stick on sunny days and stop that silly squinting.

Tulum is quite a popular place with hippies, and we saw many mega beards, topknots and miles of self-cleaning hair, to say nothing of the piercings and tattoos. Consequently, there is some artistic graffiti to be enjoyed, with one young couple sweating away on a very hot and sunny wall every time we went by creating a veritable Banksy. Good job the owners of the wall didn't suspect anything...

We did some more beach walking that day, which took our overall total to a conservative 70 miles for the day (or so it felt).

On the way back to our place we passed an old-fashioned barber's with an even more old-fashioned barber's chair. We asked if we could photograph it and he said of course, and then volunteered that it was 140 years old. I thought I could remember it from my childhood! Drew Pritchard would have given his eye teeth for it.

That night was relatively peaceful except for the ... well, you know the picture ... and next morning we boarded the bus to our final stop on this little excursion, the island of Holbox on the Gulf of Mexico.

Crowded Beaches, Tardy Plumbers and Odin the Fisherman

My Valentine's present to Jilly was nine days on a white sand island in the Gulf of Mexico, complete with blue sea and waving palm trees. I don't do these things by half, you know. Jilly gently reminded me I'd had no idea the 14th of February had any particular significance until somebody mentioned it the day before, but it was worth a try.

The comfortable bus left on time, as usual, and stopped briefly in Playa del Carmen to pick up more passengers before taking a dead straight newish toll road with hardly any traffic directly to the port of Chiquila. A half hour ferry ride brought us to Isla

Holbox. We'd been there before and loved it, so we were glad to be back.

This time we were staying in an Airbnb studio apartment. When we eventually found a lady called Minerva, who acts as a sort of housekeeper, to let us in we were very pleased with the size and layout of the place. It was only a minute's walk to our favourite bit of beach and cost £32 a night. But then we hit a few snags: although they knew what time we were arriving and Enrique, the owner, had assured us that all would be ready, the place hadn't been cleaned after the last guests, so we had to wait around whilst they spruced up. Then we found plumbing leaks with the kitchen sink waste pipe; there were no pans, nearly all the cups and plates were cracked, there was a light bulb missing and the settee was broken. We sent an email to Enrique asking for help.

We went out for a walk down the beach, found a watering hole, and bought a few basic food items. We had only been back in the apartment for a few minutes when there was a knock on the door and there was Minerva to respond to our email. She took away all the dodgy crockery and returned soon after with her son and some decent Pyrex stuff. Then she explained that they would exchange the broken settee with one from the adjoining studio, so the son took one end and Minerva tried to take the other but struggled. Muggins stepped in to help and we did the swap. One day it's pushing squeaky wheelbarrows full of coconuts, the next it's moving furniture – what kind of a holiday is this?

Minerva explained in fluent Spanish that the plomero would be round tomorrow at 10am to fix the sink. We were impressed with the speed of the response.

Well, it didn't last. Next day we waited in all morning, but the plumber didn't turn up, so I sent another email to Enrique to say we were fed up with waiting and then we made our way to Punta Coco at the western end of the island to do a bit of fishing off the beach. This is a fairly remote spot: it's a nature reserve, with no hotels or houses on the beach. Some rarish birds nest on the ground here, and there's a sea eagle's nest on a nearby power cable post. I've looked for the rarish birds' nests but never found one – which is a shame, as I'm partial to a fresh egg…

So there's the missus doing her Pilates to get shot of the last of her ricked back and I'm knee deep in the drink fishing for supper. Not a soul to be seen for the first half hour and then a young couple come around the point until they get to Jilly. With miles of empty beach in both directions they decide to settle down not ten feet from us. Fifteen minutes later another couple turn up and bugger me if they don't settle down right next to the first lot! Maybe it's a Mexican thing. The fishing was good, so we kept two for dinner.

Later that evening Minerva turned up with a light bulb, but it was the wrong size. Minutes later she returned with the right one but Muggins had to fit it as she was too short – more work! She promised the plumber would be round at 9am next morning, and to our amazement he was, but it soon became obvious that he wasn't much good. After a while he muttered "Regresso," got on his motorbike and puttered off, only to return shortly afterwards with some new parts which he tried to fit but failed, so there was another "Regresso" and another trip to his supplier. Finally, using the last dregs of an ancient tube of mastic, he told us the leak was fixed but not to use the sink for two hours whilst the mastic set.

When he disappeared, we walked the 10 minutes into town, but the minute we got there the heavens opened. We found a bar to shelter in, but Jilly decided not to wait for the rain to stop and went off shopping, only to return a little later soaked to the skin and cold. So we found a touristy clothes shop and bought the first top that fitted her, just to get her warm again.

By the afternoon the skies were blue again, so we had a long beach walk, a drink in our favourite bar and then returned to the apartment to find that the plumbing was still leaking. I fired off another email to Enrique saying we weren't prepared to waste another morning of our precious holiday waiting for the plumber and maybe Minerva could get off her a*** and let him in, to which Enrique replied that they would do just that.

Next day was a spring tide. The weather was perfect, so we had a fabulous walk along the exposed sandbank revealed by the extra low tide, which ran for at least two miles parallel to the shore and was lapped by the clearest water, with constantly changing shades of emerald. Pelicans and razorbills dived into the calm sea and the ever-vigilant frigate birds soared above, waiting to mug any smaller bird with a fish.

Jilly made a salad lunch of olives, avocado, lettuce and cucumber and then we walked to the rickety wooden dock to try out a new method of fishing I'd read about. It worked like a charm: two jacks obliged in as many minutes, and I thought I'd cracked it. Then there was nothing for the rest of the session. Back to the drawing board. I experimented with some realistic plastic shrimps I'd brought from England. I hooked one through the head and the fish bit the tail off, so I hooked the next one through the tail and the crafty devils bit the head off. Oh well, at least it started well.

There was a knock on the door at 7pm – Carlos the plumber to try again. A quick "Regresso" and this time it actually did the trick.

We booked a boat fishing trip with a very likeable man named Odin (!) but the fishing was poor because the high spring tide was carrying a lot of weed. However, I did manage to hook a double figure jack and, after a long fight, got it right to the side of the boat where Odin grabbed the line and tried to lift it in. Twelve pounds breaking strain line, heavier fish than that = disaster. I smiled bravely through my tears, though. And I lie a lot.

Nothing daunted, we tried again a couple of days later and it was a very different story: clear, calm sea and lots of fish of many different species. Odin made a delicious ceviche with some of the catch to end a perfect morning, and he even filleted four fish for us to take home and cook, with one going to our new American neighbour, Maureen.

Our other neighbour was a tame iguana so well camouflaged Jilly nearly tripped over him a couple of times. We also saw a raccoon on our little track.

And so the days whipped by and all of a sudden it was our last day here. We took a golf cart taxi to Punta Coca and spent a lovely morning enjoying the sun and catching five hard-fighting jacks and then a good sized puffer fish who also gave a good scrap and then did his party piece, blowing himself up with lots of grunts and then letting all the air out with a very rude noise!

Tomorrow we have to catch the early ferry back to the mainland from this little paradise, and then the bus to Cancun where we plan to while away a few hours with a leisurely lunch before the night flight to Blighty. I have a feeling we'll be back, though.

Part Four:

Postcards from
Guatemala and Belize

Mennonites, Iguanas
and Sybil's Husband

Having seen a bit of Latin America we were keen to visit some other parts of the Americas, with Belize being of particular interest because of its long association with Britain. We also arranged to hop over the border to Guatemala, as we were in the area.

We had a good flight from Gatwick to Cancun, Mexico with British Airways. We were in a row of three seats, the aisle seat being occupied by a young Italian lady called Francesca who was on her honeymoon. For some reason she couldn't get a seat next to her new husband. I had a quiet word about it with a stewardess and, five minutes later, they magically found two adjoining seats at the back for the newly-weds – which meant we had three seats to ourselves and I could get up for as many pees as I wanted (quite a few!) without disturbing anyone.

Customs and immigration in Cancun were very efficient but sadly the baggage reclaim was anything but. After thirty minutes gazing at the carousel and wishing there was an electrified wire to stop stupid people standing right up to it so nobody else could see what was coming, a single case appeared. Then nothing further for a few minutes. Then four more, and so on. It was another half hour before our cases finally turned up, by which time we'd missed the bus to Playa del Carmen and there wasn't another for an hour. We bit the bullet and forked out for a taxi as it had been a pretty long day. Jilly was still recovering from a severe dose of flu some five weeks earlier, so it was important to save her energy wherever possible.

We stayed overnight in a very basic hotel that's probably best forgotten. Next day, we took a taxi to 5th Avenue in Playa, which is a place we'd been to before and greatly enjoyed. It's a two-mile pedestrian-only street running parallel to the sea and lined with bars, restaurants, shops and – best of all – people. The people watching is exceptionally good there; we just sat in the hot January sun with a drink, watching the non-stop parade of eccentrics passing by. The cruise ships put in at Playa so there are always loads of tourists from all over the world (but mostly USA or Canada), and some are priceless. The bar staff try to entice them in with lines like, "Hey senor, why don't you come in for a drink, so we can rip you off?!"

We had a pleasant restful time there and then walked down the huge white beach, found some sun loungers attached to a bar where a cheery group of musicians were playing, and soaked up some rays for a couple of hours before more 5th Avenue ambling and a leisurely al fresco dinner in perfect temperatures.

The next day we caught the bus back to Cancun airport and jumped on a little plane owned by Maya Island Airlines (surely you MUST have heard of them?). It had 34 seats, of which 19 were occupied, and all the propellers worked, which was a nice surprise. As we flew south for an hour and five minutes, we had superb views of the Caribbean coast, with the Meso-American coral reef, the second largest in the world, displaying a myriad of gorgeous colours far below. We landed in Belize City, where baggage reclaim was swift as only six passengers got off – the rest were going on to Honduras. We had originally intended to bus down to Belize, but it would have taken over eight hours, so in view of Jilly's condition we splashed out on the flight and were really glad we did.

Outside the sleepy airport there were two people

waiting for incoming passengers. One young lady, with very curly hair, was holding a sign reading 'Andrew Robinson' and we waved to her as we came out. "Hello," she said, "I'm Curly," which somehow didn't seem necessary! She drove us for ninety minutes to our next destination, the town of San Ignacio, and to the Midas Resort, where, to our delight, we found we'd been upgraded to their poshest bungalow. As well as being very spacious, it had a big porch with easy chairs and a hammock at the front, and beautiful views over the valley. At the back there was a huge bay window only feet away from dense forest. Lots of wildlife to be seen. At the front there were lots of big trees and from these a succession of iguanas of all sizes could be seen marching up and down. The downward lot proceeded slowly until they hit the ground, then rushed across the lawn and into the tall reeds beyond. We saw squawking parrots flying over, kingfishers, squirrels, bright yellow flycatchers, scarlet headed woodpeckers, vultures keeping a beady eye on Jilly, herons, geckos, egrets and lots of birds that we didn't recognise at all.

We really took it easy that first week. We spent a lot of time on the porch watching the wildlife and chatting to the staff. The Belizeans are a lovely mixture of Spanish, African and Mayan, with lots of interesting combinations of the three plus a fair bit of British as this country used to be British Honduras.

They mostly have English as their first language, then Spanish and then Creole. Everyone we met was absolutely charming and kind, and I suppose a little naive in terms of looking after tourists. For instance, I wanted some worms to go fishing and one of the gardeners offered to dig some up for me. Off we went in his pickup truck to his house on the other side of town, where he introduced me to his two pit bull terriers, dug up some worms and drove me back to Midas. He wouldn't take any money for this. Just as well, because the worms didn't work.

Talking of fishing, there was a beautiful river about 10 minutes' walk down a tree-lined track and most evenings we went down there to do a bit of fishing and enjoy the scenery. The river teems with little roach-like fish in the shallows, but the big boys are few and far between. I got one good-sized one – caught the first time I tried – so, full of confidence, I invited orders from the staff and of course I failed to catch any more. I got some good bites, but after a while I realised it was turtles chomping away on the bait. Still, it was very restful down on the river bank. The only thing missing – apart from the fish – was a comfortable seat for Jilly, so we walked into town to buy her one. The only thing we could find that was remotely suitable was one of those plastic garden chairs, and after haggling with the Pakistani shopkeeper (It seems people come to Belize from all over the world!) we managed to agree on a fair price.

I gave him some money and he went off to get change. Meanwhile, a very pregnant lady with a baby decided that our chair was just what she needed for a nice sit down, so, rather than disturb her, we picked out another one and quickly left before more squatters moved in.

On our first day in Belize we went to the Saturday market, which was full of colour – both in the fruit and veg, and characters galore, including Mennonites. No, not those snail-like fossils. Mennonites are a bit like the Amish, somehow locked in a time warp. The menfolk were dressed in blue denim dungarees and wide straw hats and had great big beards; the little boys were in identical garb (but no beards) and the women looked like extras from 'Little House on the Prairie'. They speak German between themselves and over the last couple of centuries have moved from country to country because they refuse to fight; every time their latest 'home' gets into a war and they're called up they politely decline and move on, taking with them their considerable farming skills and their 18th century way of life.

After lunch I fancied a bit of kayaking in our local river. The resort had a boat we could use, but the only means of getting it to the river, ten minutes away, was by wheelbarrow, so we duly borrowed one from my gardener friend, put the kayak on and walked it down to the river. I had a lovely two hours of paddling upstream, enjoying the peace and quiet and trying hard not to think too much of 'Deliverance', although the theme music kept running through my head.

San Ignacio is bordered by the river and forests and the town itself has an interesting mixture of architectural styles which at first glance looks a little like old New Orleans, with lots of balconies. Traffic is a bit chaotic, pavements virtually non-existent, and most vehicles seem to be big American pickup trucks and 4-wheel drives. They even have old US school buses and some huge American trucks. The people, who have delightful Caribbean accents, are all very laid back and they all seem to know each other and stop for a chat. We noticed that nearly everyone we passed said hello, which was nice.

One day I was walking into town (about 10 minutes from Midas) when a topless black man with white hair came trotting along on a horse. He stopped next to me and said, "Hello, how are you?"

"Fine," I said, "how are you?"

"Pretty good," he replied, "but my horse eats a lot and grain is expensive and I could do with a loan of $60 - can you help?"

"No," I said, at which, in his lilting accent, he very courteously wished me a nice day and trotted off into the sunset. I've never come across a beggar on horseback before.

On our first night here, we walked into town for

dinner and found a quiet little Italian restaurant where a man in his 60s, dressed in shorts, was dropping cutlery all over the place. We went in and discovered he was English, married to a Guatemalan lady who was soon to bear his child. He gave us the menu but then explained that all the beef dishes were off because the meat delivered wasn't up to standard, so I ordered chicken, but this was off as well. This left a choice of about four things, so the meal wasn't very exciting, but he was such a comical character; he reminded us both of Basil Fawlty. Then he confided in us that he was running from the UK tax man. By a strange coincidence, he'd been born in the same Rustington nursing home as our son, Dan, and he'd worked on a double-glazing contract in Swindon, where we come from. He showed great concern for Jilly's health and offered to make her soup, which is about all she was enjoying at the time. We returned the following evening and he was as good as his word.

We visited a local Mayan ruin, which was pleasantly sited up in the hills, complete with semi-excavated pyramids amidst the forest. What we particularly liked about it were the pyramid shapes still completely covered in foliage, just waiting to reveal their secrets. We were both dying to get stuck in with a spade! It was all very peaceful – until an American tour group caught up with us.

Hidden Cities, Cobbled Towns and Monkeys Galore

Next day we made the short 8-mile journey to the Guatemalan border. As we went through Belize customs the official looked at our passports and asked: "How's Auntie Betty?" How on earth did he know Jilly's mother, we wondered. Then he explained that that's what the Belizeans call Queen Elizabeth, which was very sweet.

We changed some money at the border and my confusion reached an all-time high, with a wallet containing Mexican pesos, Belizean dollars, US dollars, a bit of UK sterling and now Guatemalan quetzales! Sounds more like a disease. Anyway, we took a taxi to the little town of El Remate, about an hour and a half away, or so the driver told us. I'd previously worked out that it was only 40 miles, and the road looked excellent, so I thought we'd be there in under an hour, but after ten miles the shiny new road became a potholed nightmare and we crawled along for the rest of the journey. The driver explained that all the money for the new road had gone into the pockets of el Presidente. However, we were very impressed by our first glimpse of Guatemala, which was green and cultivated, with lots of grazing cows and horses – far more than we'd seen in Belize.

We arrived at La Casa De Don David in El Remate and were knocked out by the views. If you care to Google it, you'll see that it's on the shore of the enormous Lake Peten Itza, and the restaurant at La Casa was the perfect place to take in the lake's amazing sunsets, which kept getting more and more colourful just when you thought it was over.

We saw local women up to their waists in the calm water, washing clothes and chatting to each other. How charming, we thought; nothing can have changed for centuries. Then one of the ladies turned to face us and we realised they were chatting on their mobiles. Another shattered illusion!

The owner of the property, Don David, was an old American who spoke in a quavering southern accent. He wanted to show us some tarantulas that allegedly lived in a rockery near our room, but none appeared, to our relief. He noticed that we'd left our door open to air the place, but he wasn't too happy about that. "You only gotta leave your door open for a minute for a skeeter to fly in, then you got yourself a sleepless night tryin' to slap him for hours." Good point.

We chose this place because of its beautiful position and also because it's the nearest village to Tikal, which is one of the most important Mayan sites. At 5.30 next morning we duly climbed into a minibus to take us to the site, and an hour later we were walking through the jungle in the misty dawn light. Almost immediately we spotted a large guinea pig-like rodent called an agouti, and then we heard what we'd hoped to hear - the roar of howler monkeys. They continued to shatter the peace for the next twenty minutes as we gradually climbed upwards and the light became better.

After half an hour we still hadn't seen any Mayan ruins, but suddenly, out of the mist a vast temple emerged, and after that we came across more and more impressive ruins in various stages of excavation. Just as the sun showed itself through the mist, we arrived at the Gran Plaza, a large open square area surrounded by massive buildings, towers and pyramids. I climbed a pyramid and watched from the top as Jilly did sun salutations far below. There were only a few people about at that early hour, but then three yobs appeared with a blaring transistor radio and ruined the peace. They ignored the signs about not climbing the steps and had bellowed conversations over the row coming from the radio. I am a peaceful man but how I wished that they could have become the next sacrificial victims in that ancient place. I would have gladly ripped their still beating hearts out of their bodies and hurled them down from the top of the pyramid – or is that over-reacting?

We walked around the vast site for many hours, stopping only for water breaks and a packed lunch, which had to be abandoned for a while as a troop of monkeys in the trees above us kept throwing sticks down at us. If it's not yobs, it's bloody monkeys! We also saw jungle turkeys with blue heads, and many other exotic birds, trees and plants. We found the tallest temple at 65 metres and I climbed the 175 steps to what I thought was going to be the top, but there was nearly as much again above me when I got there, although it was too unsafe to venture further. What a view from where I was, though, far above the forest canopy, with the tops of other temples peeping through the trees and a jungle vista stretching for miles and miles all around.

Next day we caught the chicken bus to the town of Santa Elena, en route to Flores. The old bus was absolutely crammed with people, or so we thought, but having somehow wedged us huge gringos in, the bus kept stopping for more and more and each time we had to scramble out so that the driver could re-pack the multitudes, and then somehow squeeze us in again. The bus had to weave from one side of the road to the other to avoid the potholes but after an hour or so, we were spat out in Santa Elena where the ride ended. We then opted to walk in the heat through the town on what was market day, so you can imagine how busy it was with frenetic traffic, cops blowing whistles, Mexican-type music blaring from speakers, tethered chickens on the pavement, market stalls bulging with colourful, exotic produce and every other bloke dressed like a cowboy in white Stetson and jeans. Our walk took us down the hill to the same huge lake we'd left that morning and over a causeway to the lovely island town of Flores, which is as quiet and quaint as its sister town, Santa Elena, is brash and noisy. Here the narrow streets are cobbled and lined with brightly painted cottages and shops, as well as restaurants with balconies giving great views of the blue lake all around. Little boats ferry people to and fro, either commuting to the mainland to work or just for pleasure, and the weather was very warm indeed.

We were staying in a place called Casazul; we were on the second floor and had a very big verandah overlooking the lake. We had a lovely, lazy time on the island, ambling about, doing a bit of shopping and taking a lot of tea breaks to cool down and enjoy the views. When I say tea breaks, that only applies to Jilly. A cold beer fits the bill as far as I'm concerned.

We woke up early the following morning, which was not surprising as there was a firework display at 5am. We never did find out why.

We went for a boat trip around our part of the lake and saw a chap in a dugout canoe catch a nice big fish called, he told us, a blanco, although it didn't look white. In fact, it was very like the fish I caught in the river at San Ignacio, with vertical stripes and a big spot near the tail. Maybe the flesh is white. Anyway, it was a lovely relaxing ride with great views of Flores from the water.

Next day we were off to the seaside for a well-deserved break after all this physical effort!

Speed Bumps, Jacks
and Johnny Cake

We left Flores on a minibus headed for southern Belize. The driver and his mate never stopped talking the whole way to the border. Trouble was, the driver was one of those people who can't talk to someone without looking at them, so he drove most of the way looking at his mate rather than the road. Nonetheless, we arrived at the Belize border without incident and were fleeced on the exchange rate when we changed our remaining Guatemalan quetzales into Belize dollars.

A taxi ride took us back to San Ignacio, where we'd left our main luggage in storage. As soon as we got out of the taxi we spotted Nigel, the Basil Fawlty character from the Italian restaurant, and, simultaneously, another chap we knew, so it felt a bit like coming home.

We picked up our luggage and took the bus to Dangriga, a small town on the Caribbean noted for its population of Garifuna, a race of people descended from escaped African slaves who palled up with the last of the Caribs on one of the islands before being deported by the British to an island off Honduras, where most of them starved to death. Eventually, the survivors were shipped to Belize to work in the logging industry. They speak their own language as well as Creole and English and are famous for their drumming expertise. Not many people know that.

The bus came to a stop and a beaming young woman got on carrying a big tray. In that lovely lilting Caribbean accent, she shouted: "Hello everyone, delicious freshly baked cakes and bread for sale!" Soon the bus was filled with the smell of freshly baked cakes and bread, oddly enough. We weren't hungry, but it seemed as though everyone else was, as she was sold out in minutes and got off the bus at the next stop.

In Dangriga the plan was to catch another bus to take us to the village of Placencia. It turned out we'd missed our connection and there wasn't another bus for two hours, so we befriended a Canadian couple who were in the same predicament and clubbed together for a taxi. There had recently been a smart new road built to Placencia but for some reason they'd installed huge sleeping policemen every quarter of a mile. With five people in the car plus our combined luggage, we had to slow to a crawl at every speed bump and even then, the exhaust pipe caught on the road every time. It was a long and excruciating journey, with us expecting the exhaust to be ripped off each time we hit a bump.

Placencia appears in the Guinness Book of Records for having the narrowest main street in the world – a four-feet wide concrete ribbon that runs for about a mile through the village. However, it's a bit of a cheat as there's also a proper road running parallel that takes the vehicular traffic.

Placencia is Spanish for peace, and peaceful it certainly was. The resort lies on the end of a 20-mile sand spit with a lagoon on one side and the Caribbean on the other, and it certainly felt as though we'd come to the end of the road in the nicest possible sense. Everything is laid back and everyone seems to know each other. People smile and greet each other, including us tourists, so we felt very welcome. The houses are painted in bright Caribbean colours which would look awful in Britain but are somehow just right here. The beach seems to stretch on forever and is composed of golden sand about the texture of granulated sugar, and it's so deep it's not possible to walk fast on it, so nobody does. Take it easy, man.

We finally arrived at about four in the afternoon and checked into the Seaspray, which was right on the beach. As soon as we'd dumped our bags in the room, we walked the 50 yards to the sea like excited kids. And there, only 100 yards out, was a school of dolphins waiting to greet us.

We saw the dolphins most days, which was a joy, and then one day we thought at first we were looking at them again but as they surfaced, we realised we were seeing manatees. We also saw pelicans and frigate birds, hummingbirds in the flowering trees around the hotel and various other pretty birds we didn't recognise.

I went fishing from the beach at dawn every morning for an hour, and then tried again at sunset. The first time I'd only been fishing for ten minutes when I caught a nice fish called a jack. It fought really well, but I put it back. The second evening I hooked a much bigger fish that took me all over the place for five minutes before everything went slack. I guessed a barracuda had got in on the action and bitten through the line. But, 20 minutes later, I hooked another big fish that had me racing down the beach to keep up with him. Eventually I beached him; another jack of about 6lbs! I took him to the restaurant next door for our dinner that night. Can't get much fresher than that.

By now Jilly had virtually recovered from her bout of the flu. Most mornings she did yoga on the beach under a shady palm tree but was a bit wary of falling coconuts. We took some lovely walks along the beach and she'd finally got her appetite back. She even brought me coffee when I was fishing at dawn. I just need to train her to bring red wine in the evening as well!

The supermarkets are very quaint here. They're not very big and are all run by Chinese, but they stock things like tins of Spam and Tide washing powder: lots of old-fashioned British products that just seem bizarre to see in faraway Belize. We had a kitchenette in our room, so we bought some Spam, apples and pears, a very tasty hard cheese they make over here, bread and margarine and used these ingredients to concoct a sort of anglicised tapas lunch which we enjoyed on the beach.

We hired a kayak and went for a paddle round the lagoon one morning. Very pleasant, gently creeping up on fishing herons and seeing kingfishers launch themselves from the mangrove branches. I tried fishing from the kayak a couple of times, but the barracuda kept biting the tails off the soft plastic lures I was using, which rendered them useless.

The food here is mostly fresh from the sea, and I was hooked on shrimp dishes. Well, they call them shrimps, but we'd call them prawns. Because they mostly cater for Americans the portions are very generous, and sometimes it was a real struggle to eat all those succulent shrimps – but somehow, I managed it. Jilly enjoyed veggie dishes although she was starting to eat fish now she was feeling better.

We tended to eat at the restaurant next door to our hotel, because it was right on the beach and the food was excellent. However, this being Belize, there was the occasional hiccup. One night they ran out of red wine. Unforgivable! The 'front of house' man, Fred, was responsible for ordering stock as well as charming the punters, but unfortunately, he was worse than hopeless. He never spoke to a customer unless he absolutely had to and avoided all eye contact. He appeared to spend most of his time playing patience on the computer and, we were reliably informed, organising secret poker games. As far as we could see he had no interest whatsoever in the restaurant and it showed – because they ran out of wine a second time, too.

One Belizean dish we were keen to try was fry jacks, and we ordered a typical local breakfast which included stuffed fry jacks. It was like Yorkshire pudding but filled with chopped bacon, eggs, tomatoes and something slightly spicy. Very different, but actually quite tasty and very filling – I didn't eat another thing until dinner.

Another famous local dish is the Johnny cake, but every time I ordered one they'd run out, so it became a bit of an obsession to track one down. We joked that being a Johnny cake it might be a bit rubbery, but when we finally got some, they turned out to be what we used to call dampers in the Scouts. Made from flour and water as a patty, you could use them like bread with the main course or spread jam on them.

The weather in Belize is quite changeable; whilst it's always warm, it does tend to start off very still in the mornings, and just as the sun gets higher and it's on the verge of feeling too hot a welcome breeze springs up, growing stronger by the hour, so by evening the sea is fairly rough. This means flotsam is blown onto the beach, and as well as weed we noticed lots of pumice stone on the tide wrack. Lord knows where it comes from; some distant volcano or undersea eruption, presumably.

After a wonderful few days in Placencia, we were heading back to Dangriga where we hoped to find a certain cafe and ask for Captain Buck, who would, we hoped, take us to a tiny speck of a coral island for the next stage of our adventure.

Captain Buck, Two Jolly Ladies
and a Beach Party

Placencia backs onto a huge lagoon and on the other side is the village of Independence, whose only claim to fame is that it offered a better route to where we were going next than the speed-bump-plagued road. The only way to get to Independence from Placencia is to catch the Hokey Pokey, which is the quirky name of the boat that serves the two communities. The boat races along at 40mph across the open lagoon and then, without losing speed, twists and turns through a network of mangrove-flanked channels. It's an exciting 10-minute ride, a bit like being in a James Bond chase scene.

We caught the express bus back to the town of Dangriga and had a pleasant journey through flat countryside framed by the Mayan mountains. Oddly for such a hot country, there were a lot of Scots pines initially, and then we came to banana plantations and citrus groves, which were a lot more tropical. We passed little farming communities where the people lived in thatched cottages.

Dangriga is a gritty working town on an estuary, populated almost entirely by the Garifuna people, many sporting Rasta hairstyles; we were a bit apprehensive there to start with. We walked from the bus station for some ten minutes until we reached the Riverside café, where we were supposed to rendezvous with Captain Buck at high noon; he was to take us to the island of Tobacco Caye (pronounced 'key'). We were far too early, so we had breakfast there and sat outside in the sun on the river bank, watching the world go by and working on a limerick about Captain Buck.

Pelicans lined the river waiting for the fishermen to finish cleaning their catch and throw the leftovers out for them. We watched a fight narrowly averted between a large Rasta who was knocking back the rum and another dubious-looking gentleman. We even went for a wander around the outdoor market on the opposite bank and generally enjoyed our people watching.

Eventually, Captain Buck appeared. He was of

African heritage, short and stocky with a grey beard and extremely bloodshot eyes. He explained that he had some shopping to do for the island, so he'd be another hour or so. He issued instructions to various bods who then set off to different shops and came back laden with veg, meat, fruit, loo rolls, fuel, bottled water and booze. Absolutely everything had to be transported to the island and his was the only boat. While he waited for various goods to turn up, we saw him take the odd sneaky nip of something from a small bottle to keep his spirits up. Finally, all the purchases plus us and our luggage were loaded into the 20-foot open boat and we motored down the river to where it met the sea. Buck and his mate had to hop out into the water to push the overloaded boat over the shallow bar and into deeper water before climbing in again and setting off for the island.

There was a strong headwind, so Captain Buck told us to get under the large tarpaulin and pull it over us. We sat facing the rear of the boat and peeped out as Buck got wetter and wetter, snarling in defiance as great showers of seawater hit him in the face. He didn't look at all happy. But 30 minutes later the boat stopped its crashing through the waves as we approached our little island, bathed in sunshine and decorated with waving palms. We waved back. It seemed only polite.

Our luggage was rapidly whisked to our cabin by a chap with a wheelbarrow (the only form of transport on the island) and we set off to explore our new land. It took about ten minutes all told, as the island is only the size of a football pitch. There were two bars, several wooden docks in various states of repair, a snack shop and a dining room attached to our cabins, where we had a lunch of delicious chowder prepared by two very jolly ladies. The deal was that we had three meals a day included in the price of our accommodation, which was £60 a day for the two of us. That evening, dinner was lobster Thermidor and we began to think we might have got a good deal. All meals were announced by the clanging of a bell, and there was unlimited coffee and tea in the mornings.

The island has hammocks strung between the coconut palms and lots of brightly painted wooden chairs on the docks and beaches. The sea was a kaleidoscope of different shades of blue. The weather was always warm and during the four days we stayed there it got better and better. The island is right on the Meso-American Reef (the second largest in the world after the Barrier Reef) and we could snorkel right off the beach over coral with lots of pretty fish – and a few scary ones. The water is so clear, we saw stingrays and eagle rays when we were just standing on the dock. On one of the docks there is an abandoned wooden hut that used to be a dive shop, and on its roof was an ospreys' nest, complete with resident ospreys.

Our cabin had everything we needed: a big paddle fan on the ceiling, a second free-standing fan, a fridge and an en suite with hot and cold taps. Sadly, none of these modern miracles worked except the cold tap, but it was spacious, with two double beds and a big verandah right on the beach, so we could always hear the sea. We were very happy there – apart from the bloody cold showers! I used to scream a lot before my tender body got used to it.

I went fishing off the reef and caught barracuda and snappers, all of which were served up to us and our fellow guests by the brilliant jolly ladies. One day, a party yacht moored overnight and there was a bit of drunken revelry (no, not me) as the crew enjoyed themselves, which was no big deal but next day, when they'd sailed off, we found that they'd drunk all the beer on the island. Even worse, they'd also drunk all the red wine (why are people so selfish?) so Captain Buck was despatched on a top priority mercy mission to replenish the stocks of booze. We think he'd been on the rum again, because when he got back, he'd got the beer and the plonk, but he'd been instructed to buy Baileys as well and he'd bought loo rolls instead. Well, it's close...

One morning I went out fishing with a local called George, a grizzled veteran and probably the grumpiest man in the world. He knew his fishing, though, and although we only went a little way offshore, we had a lot of fun. We went in an ancient, much patched fibreglass canoe and paddled too close for comfort near the rocky reef, where big waves were pounding. I sat in front and was responsible for the anchor, which consisted of a whacking great breeze block on the end of a rope. We dropped anchor, which nearly capsized us with the sudden switch of weight, and George told me exactly where to cast. In the unstable, bobbing canoe I got it wrong a couple of times and got a right tongue lashing, but then I hit the spot and caught several fish he called pargy, which have deep bodies and are very powerful. Then something picked up the bait and went off like a train in the direction of Cuba. I couldn't hold it and it continued its journey unimpeded by the likes of me, but still, it was very exciting stuff in such a flimsy boat. And I got another bollocking from George for losing it! George filleted the pargy when we got back to land, and we had them for dinner that night. They were truly excellent eating and there was enough for everybody.

The sun rose in front of our cabin and set on the other side of the island, but it was worth the long walk (two minutes) to watch it set over the Caribbean, sitting in a comfy chair with a cool drink and enjoying the balmy evening air.

There were literally thousands of conch shells on the island (you know, the great big curly ones the natives use as trumpets). You can see the live ones trundling about in the shallows and they make good eating and even better bait, so they're a much-prized catch. However, there are small mountains of the empty shells on some parts of the island and they even build walls with them. I discovered that if you hold an empty one to your ear you can actually hear the sea...

Jilly, feeling much better now, continued doing yoga on the beach. One day a new couple from America arrived; the wife happened to be a yoga teacher. There was an Italian couple as well, and we all got on so well together that we had an impromptu party on the Italians' verandah that night, pooling our resources. We contributed biscuits, nuts and a very squashed fruit bar that had somehow come with us from England; the Americans provided whiskey and weed and two of the party decided to eat cereal with watered down evaporated milk that one of them had somehow conjured up. As it was our last night and some were a trifle merry, it seemed like a good idea for Sam, the yoga teacher, to hold a class at sunrise next morning. I managed to avoid this as I had to pay the bill. The others enjoyed it, I think.

And so we reluctantly left the island and had a dry ride back with Captain Buck who was, as usual, as miserable as sin. We made sure we were on the dock in good time because Buck doesn't wait for anybody. Some people made the mistake of being a wee bit late and he went without them, so they had to stay another night. He was quite a character.

Giants, Slebs
and The Island of Women

Back on the mainland, we caught the bus to Belize City. This time it was an ancient US school bus with no aircon. All the windows were open, so we looked a bit windswept by the time we arrived at the halfway stop, which was the world's smallest capital city, Belmopan. It's a fairly recently created 'city' in the middle of nowhere, which houses the administrative centre and government of the country. Nobody wants to live there unless they have to, so the population is only about 15,000. Its name is a combination of the first syllable of Belize and the word Mopan, the name of the principal river, which in turn is named after the Mopan Maya, who were the original inhabitants of the country and are still very much in evidence. Lots of obscure quiz material there!

We had a ten-minute toilet break in Belmopan, during which a chap got on the bus and sat down a couple of seats in front of us, followed a few minutes later by an enormous man who screamed threats at the first bloke. I thought we were in for a punch up, if not a murder, but the first man wisely said nothing and the giant ran out of steam and stamped off, the whole bus shaking as he went.

We set off on the last leg of the journey, which was mostly downhill. We were travelling pretty fast when all of a sudden the brakes were slammed on and the bus swerved violently to one side, over-corrected and swerved to the other. People were screaming (or was it only me?). Just when it seemed certain that the bus was going to overturn the driver managed to regain control and all the passengers burst into spontaneous applause, shouting in their delightful accents, "Well done, de driver!" We never seem to get all this added entertainment on National Express coaches. The cause of the excitement appeared to be a car that was swerving all over the road; we assume the driver was either drunk or drugged.

Belize City needs to be handled with caution. Situated on an estuary, it's by far the biggest place in

Belize (70,000 population) and is the main port of access for the two most popular holiday islands. Americans and Canadians fly into Belize City airport and taxi to the port, where water taxis wait to whisk them off to their chosen island. However, there's a high crime rate in the city so few tourists choose to stay there, and those who do are warned not to walk around on their own after dark.

We arrived in daylight, dumped our bags at the hotel and walked along the waterfront to stretch our legs. As we crossed the bridge to get to the port, we became more and more aware of what a dodgy place it was, even in the sunshine. Lots of idle young men stared at us malevolently and there were a few beggars in the seedy streets. In general, there was a lot of tension in the air.

We were heading for the port because it looked jolly from our hotel across the river, but when we got there, we found it was securely fenced off from the city and the guards wanted ID, so we showed them our passports. They wanted to keep them as security, but Jilly was having none of it, so they asked me for my driving licence instead. I handed over my tattered, 30-year-old licence but they said it was no good because it didn't have a photo on it. Well, we were hot and tired after our lengthy journey and I was desperate for a beer, so I told him to forget it, we'd go somewhere else – at which point he decided that two old codgers probably weren't going to break his precious dock and just waved us through. Isn't common sense marvellous?

We found a bar up some stairs with a great view of all the tourists below and enjoyed an hour or so of watching our American cousins whooping it up as they waited for their boats. Then we headed back to our nice little hotel before it got dark and the vampires emerged.

Next day we cheated again and took the same Mayan Island Airline propeller plane we'd come on to whisk us back to Cancun, Mexico; this time there were only ten passengers on board. I can't see this airline lasting too long with that sort of footfall. Again, the views of the coastline were spectacular, and an hour later we were back in Mexico, where we experienced something very odd at Customs and Immigration. When we stepped off the plane, we were all told to line up and wait while a uniformed lady took photos of us. Another official collected our passports and walked off with them. He returned after ten minutes and shouted out the name on each passport. As we each claimed our passport we were photographed individually and then we were allowed to go. No explanation, no apology. We wondered if they were looking for somebody, but we'll probably never know what it was all about.

From the airport we took a shuttle van to the port and then a ferry to our next and final resort, Isla Mujeres (Island of Women). We'd been there before on our first trip to Mexico to escape from the all-inclusive hell that is Cancun. It was a laid-back little island with pretty beaches that we'd both loved, and although we rarely go back to the same place twice, we were happy to make an exception for Isla Mujeres. The ferry trip lasts 30 minutes and takes you through the most amazing sea colours we've ever seen. There was a busker playing a medley of songs, which made it even more enjoyable.

The island is long and narrow, with the town at one end where we were staying. The following day we hired a golf cart for the day and drove right round the island, which only took 90 minutes. We enjoyed it so much that we did it again! Then we had a leisurely lunch and a bit of beach time.

A jolly bunch of Americans and Canadians were staying at our hotel, all pals, and they welcomed us into the gang and invited us to join them at Happy Hour for a walk around the town. The town is small, with the docks on one side, into which come the frequent ferries plus a succession of party boats from Cancun that disgorge their passengers for seafood lunches and beer or cocktails, then whip them off for a bit of a cruise and some boozy games. It's fun to watch from a distance. However, a couple of blocks away there are quiet side streets and a long, pedestrian-only section with bars, restaurants and shops that's filled at night with buskers, men dressed as Mayan warriors, fire eaters, tap dancers etcetera.

We ate in various places – posh Italian to hole in the wall Mexican, Texan and Thai, you name it – and the food was always good to excellent.

Jilly found a fairly secluded beach close by our hotel where she liked to do her yoga, and I went for a morning's fishing with one of our new American friends from the hotel. Our boat was pulled over by the marine police boat, complete with flashing lights and siren. There was a long conversation in rapid fire Spanish about whether our boat had the correct licence, which it had, so off we went again. We hooked and lost a few barracuda and the American struggled with a very big fish, which had grabbed the yellow tail snapper that had taken his lure. Sadly, the barracuda let go and the snapper came in virtually ripped in half. We saw a few turtles and enjoyed the warmth and the gorgeous sea colours over the reefs. We had a good time even though we didn't catch much.

All too soon it was time to leave, and we arranged a transfer from the mainland port direct to the airport. The deal was that we paid a $10 deposit and the van would meet us at the port in a specified place and time. He never turned up, so we had to grab a cab in the end, but we arrived at the airport in good time and had an excellent flight back to chilly England. Whilst we were waiting for baggage reclaim one of those electric buggies that elderly or disabled people use to get around the airports rolled up. Sitting in the back were Mr and Mrs Rolf Harris – this was, of course, before his very public fall from grace. We ended up walking through Customs together, with Mrs H lagging behind as she was a bit frail. Rolf turned around to see where she'd got to and I was so tempted to start singing 'Did you think I would leave you lying when there's room on my horse for two' – but I wasn't quite brave enough.

On reflection, we'd probably been a bit ambitious about the amount of venues we'd tried to pack in to this trip – especially with Jilly far from fit. However, we'd been able to adapt to the situation and we both had a very good time.

Part Five:

Yet More Postcards from Mexico!

Hacksaws, Sand Dunes and Jaws: The Return

There was a time when we wouldn't go back to the same place twice, but we love Mexico and there are still great chunks of this huge country that we haven't seen. This time we left our builder, Dave, knocking holes in our relatively new home and jumped on the train to Gatwick – only we jumped ship at Redhill, where we were met by nephew Joe who took us to see big sister Gill, who recently broke her leg in a fall. She looked remarkably well and it was good to see her before our long holiday.

Joe cooked a wonderful curry at his home, not knowing that Jilly is not keen on that particular dish.

However, she absolutely loved it, so I may yet be able to convert her. Joe then very kindly drove us to our hotel near the airport where we spent a peaceful night, arriving at the airport at a civilised hour the next morning ready for our once a year holiday treat: a bacon butty. We found a cafe with a spare table and ordered said butties, only to have the waitress refuse our order in no uncertain terms: "This is a Lebanese restaurant, we don't serve bacon!" A bit off, I thought, so we flounced out (well, I did; I do a good flounce) and satisfied our craving in the cafe next door.

The direct flight to Cancun with BA was uneventful, and we were lucky to have three seats to ourselves as two passengers didn't show up. Mini rant number one: having paid £100s for our seats, why do the people behind think they have divine right to haul themselves up and down by grabbing OUR seats every time they go to the loo? Rant over, but I suspect it won't be the last...

We cleared Cancun airport quickly and then were brave enough to get on the public bus to our first port of call, Puerto Morelos, about 25 minutes' drive from the airport. We love this sleepy little seaside resort and it's a good place to unwind and acclimatise after the long journey. It has miles of white sand, a clear Caribbean Sea, friendly folk, just the right amount of tourists plus lots of excellent restaurants and watering holes.

On our first night the power went, which meant we had no air conditioning, no fan and no kettle, so it got a bit warm. As dawn broke the electricity started flickering on, then off, then on again … It put us in mind of a long-ago holiday in Portugal where we were woken by what sounded like cannons firing and marching bands. The windows in our cheap room were too high to see what was going on, but we wondered if they were having another revolution. As it happened, it was just a fiesta, but the memory prompted me to try and teach Jilly the latest shortcut to Spanish I'd learned, which was that most English words ending in 'tion' are the same in Spanish, just pronounced a little differently, e.g. 'revolution' becomes 'rev-ol-oo-see-on'. "I hope not," Jilly said. "I hope it's just the electrics." We hooted with laughter for the next five minutes.

Next morning we unpacked, and then repacked our 'valuable' stuff in the suitcases for safe keeping. As I clicked the first padlock closed, I asked Jilly if she had the keys. You guessed it, they were in the case I'd just locked. So this is a good start to our holiday: kicked out of a cafe and locked out of our case! We tried everywhere in the port for a hacksaw, to no avail. About three kilometres away is what is known as the Colonia, which is the main town as opposed to the seaside resort. This is where most of the locals live and where the hardware stores and big supermarkets are, so we duly walked there, bought a big hacksaw and a new padlock and went back to our hotel to do some sawing. Not your usual holiday pursuit. We passed the saw on to the hotel handyman, who was a bit startled that strange gringos had brought a hacksaw all the way from England for him. Next time we really should buy a padlock with a combination lock, but then we'd probably forget the combination, knowing us.

Lunch was guacamole and chips and then we took a long walk along the beach, enjoying the warmth of the hot sun as our feet were slightly cooled by the clear, blue water. There are literally miles of clean, white sand and the occasional beach bar with brollies over sun beds. The people watching is great: lots of Mexicans, Americans and Canadians, and very few Europeans.

We'd brought two headlamp torches with us but the first one I tried immediately broke, and then we somehow lost the remaining one, so next day it was back to the Colonia to try and buy replacements. We walked for miles around the town. It was all very interesting and the people, as usual, smiled and murmured greetings as we passed by. Our search took us past what appeared to be a club for retired folk in the form of a tree-shaded area where the old boys sat and played backgammon whilst the women, dressed in traditional costume, practised a group dance to the music of what Jilly said was 'Mexicans Dance on Their Hats' but when we were kids we'd sing the first line as 'I'm Mexican Pete the Bad Bandit'. Anyway, it was all very enjoyable – even though we never did track down replacement torches.

Our little hotel was perfectly situated about 100 yards from the main square, with lots of shops, bars and restaurants to choose from and the sea just two blocks away. Right opposite was a Uruguayan restaurant in a beautiful garden completely hidden from the road. There I had an amazingly good entrecôte steak and very nice wine, whilst Jilly opted for pasta, but it was disappointingly bland. Then a Mexican duo set up amplifiers and held the audience spellbound, with her singing everything from jazz to bossanova to, amazingly, Vietnamese and various classics whilst he accompanied very professionally on guitar.

Another night we went to an Argentinian restaurant just around the corner on a quiet side street, with tables and chairs in the road. It had been well recommended, and Jilly's fish was good, but my steak was dreadful and I had to spit it out in the end! I complained, and they knocked a chunk off the bill, but it rather spoilt the evening. And I swear I didn't mention a word about Las Malvinas before we ate, although I was very tempted to do so as we left.

While we were there, an almost non-stop series of street performers appeared. I usually hate these because as often as not they're not very good, but that night we saw some real quality acrobatics and also a chap doing amazing things with balls(!). Then a little lad turned up and asked diners if they would like him to sing a song for them. One couple said okay, so he burst into song with the deepest voice you've ever heard from a kid whose voice had yet to break. The only trouble was, he wasn't very tuneful and the song was very long. Oh well, you win some, you lose some.

As usual, dawn and dusk found me doing a bit of fishing off the wooden pier close by, but I struggled to catch anything despite trying various methods. Then one evening something picked up the bait and just kept trundling off out to sea, with me hanging onto the rod with all my might. It was like trying to stop a tank! Inevitably it was a case of yet another one that got away. If I had to guess I would say it was a big old stingray, so it was just as well I didn't win that battle.

Our four days in Puerto Morelos drifted past very pleasantly, with long walks where we enjoyed the warmth on our bones and leisurely lunches with oh so nice margaritas or beer for me and weirdo teas for Jilly. One day we walked for over an hour past the nudist hotel (snigger snigger!) to the little place we stayed at three years ago. Just yards from the sea, it consisted of a few modest cabins and a bar/cafe sandwiched between big, posh all-inclusive resorts. The owner back then was sure he would get an offer he couldn't refuse from some mega hotel chain, so he never bothered to update anything. When we'd stayed there the sand had blown in and was gradually covering the sun beds and palapas. Three years later nothing much had changed except the sand was even deeper – we actually had to crawl under a palapa to lie on the sun lounger. Presumably no buyer yet, then.

One day at dawn I was minding my own business fishing off the dock when, just as the sun was peeping over the horizon, a young chap, off his head after partying all night, came running up the pier, narrowly missing me before diving into the sea and soaking me with spray. "Gracias, amigo!" I shouted, but he didn't give a hoot. As if that weren't bad enough, what hove into view next was a bride and groom in full regalia, closely followed by a photographer, who snapped them from all angles and in various poses as they approached me up the pier. Alert readers may remember an incident a couple of years ago when I was mugged by a similar unlikely duo. A bit like Jaws 2. Anyway, up they sidled, getting in the way of my fishing, and in the end I was so distracted by the absurdity of the situation that I missed a good bite. The fish took me into a rock and I got broken up. So soaked and fed up was I that I was packing up to go when the photographer implored me to stay as it made for a great shot. But no, I was not to be consoled and stalked off in high dudgeon (whatever that is). Moral of the story: always leave your audience wanting more.

Next stop Mexico City!

Gold, Tequila and Ants in the Sky

A comfortable two hours in a smart plane took us to Mexico City and a taxi ride later we arrived at Hotel Diligencias. They had building work going on in the reception area so it was just like home! Our room was spacious and well equipped, so we dumped our stuff and set out to explore with a street map, though not having a clue where we were. We walked into the hot sun and began to get a sense of foreboding as we were dazzled by the sun and deafened by the traffic, with car horns and sirens blaring. We came across dodgy-looking weirdos every few yards and then a group of about thirty cops standing behind riot shields.

We ducked down a quieter street and found a rather posh restaurant which was like an oasis for us: suddenly peaceful and cool, giving us time to collect our thoughts and have a drink and a snack in peace. Much refreshed, and feeling more positive, we found our way to the main city square where there was a demonstration going on at the far side, presumably the reason for the riot police. There we went into the impressive cathedral and were duly dazzled by all the gold and the colossal size of the place.

Gradually we felt more at ease with the city. We came across various impressive buildings and some street musicians, then some remains of the original Aztec city when the whole place was built on a huge lake, long since disappeared, with the Spanish conquerors using the stonework to build their own churches and mansions.

Much to our amazement, the temperature dropped like a stone that evening. For some reason we hadn't clocked that Mexico City is high, some 2250 metres, so there are big temperature differences between day and night. We then remembered that the English football team, including Bobby Moore, went there early for a World Cup in order to acclimatise. So much for my research. On reflection, the altitude coupled with the flight might have had something to do with our initial misgivings.

The main reason for coming here (apart from the fact that there wasn't much choice as most flights in

Mexico use Mexico City as their hub) was to see the enormous lost city of Teotihuacan which lies about 25 miles away, and for that we'd booked an early morning tour. We set off in the dark the next morning to the meeting place across town. The minibus picked us up and we were driven through the chaotic traffic and into the hills surrounding the city, where thousands of poorer workers live in slums and commute to the centre each day. Along the dual carriageway we passed thousands of cyclists on some sort of sponsored ride.

Rant number two: on the seat behind us were two American girls, one of whom talked non-stop for the entire journey in a grating, penetrating voice, with every other word being 'like'. Maybe she sensed my rapidly rising annoyance, because she then introduced a dramatic improvement to her vocabulary with 'kinda like'. Aargh!!!

We arrived at Teotihuacan and parked up. This massive city had already been abandoned for 600 years before the Aztecs found it and came to the conclusion that it must have been built by the gods. It centres around a three-kilometre broad, straight avenue, which is split into many walled terraces to hold any rainwater. Various impressive buildings line the avenue with the biggest by far being two stonking great pyramids, the Pyramid of the Moon and the Pyramid of – you guessed it – the Sun. Jilly made me climb the biggest one, which made me puff a bit, but I had some great views from the top. Apparently, from the ground I and the other tourists who'd made the trek looked like ants!

Every few minutes we heard loud bangs and puffs of smoke would appear in the sky. Our guide explained that there were various obscure religions that had set up close by who believed the fireworks would wake up the gods so they could help the believers.

Nobody knows who built this enigmatic place, or when, or why, as no written clues have been found so far, and nobody knows why it was abandoned all those years ago. My own private theory is that it was all that f---ing banging day and night...

As we finished hiking round the ruins, things improved dramatically with an included tequila and mescal tasting session. As Jilly doesn't drink, I bravely stepped in to try her share. There were all sorts to try: one variety needed you to squeeze a bit of lime into your mouth before trying the tequila; another had an almond taste (no, not cyanide); there were various vintages, too. The one I preferred was a mescal matured in oak barrels. The entertaining Mexican lady who introduced us to all these delights then gave a brief talk on how the drink was made and showed us how the agave plant could produce a smooth version of paper. Pity the Teotihuacan people didn't know this trick as they could have left some very nice written notes and stopped all the conjecture. Another thing she showed us was how, if you sawed around the tough spike at the tip of the leaf, you could then gently pull it off together with a long strand of strong fibre which could be used as a ready-made needle and thread. Very handy tip should you lose a button off your trousers whilst out in the Mexican desert.

We then had an excellent buffet lunch spoilt only by two dreadful singers who were followed by two girls in authentic Aztec costume (although I couldn't help noticing a blue bra strap on one of them). One of the girls did a half-hearted dance whilst the other pounded a very loud drum for absolutely ages. Meanwhile, the ancient but hyper American lady who'd joined us on our table never stopped talking whilst eating, so we were glad when it was time to get back on the bus and head back to the city.

Heads were nodding on the drive back, including, to our great delight, the, like, American, like, girl who was kinda like zonked, thank God! We arrived back in Mexico City and suddenly had to change to a different minibus as the road to the morning collection point was blocked by another demo. As we were driven along, we came to an attractive road with lovely colonial buildings facing a big, leafy square, so we got off there and had a leisurely stroll around the park. Plenty of locals were doing the same, and young men on skateboards were practising falling off, or so it seemed to us. In the nick of time we came to a pleasant, shady cafe and enjoyed a couple of drinks there whilst we watched the people parade going by.

Mexico City was beginning to grow on us, but we had no more time as we were due to fly to the Pacific Coast the next morning. Yippee!

Surfers, Dolphins and Montezuma's Revenge

Faced with the choice of twelve hours on a coach or an hour and five minutes on a plane we chickened out again and chose the quick, relatively inexpensive (£50pp) flight. We had window seats, plenty of legroom and clear visibility all the way, with fine views of the forbidding mountain range between Mexico City and the coast. They even managed to give us a complimentary drink before we arrived at our destination, Puerto Escondido on the Pacific Ocean. We made a perfect landing and taxied straight to the arrivals hall at the sleepy little airport. As we got off the plane we noticed that ours was the only one there, and after a short wait the bags came through intact.

We got taken for a ride in more ways than one with the taxi to our next home as they charged us £4 more than they should have done, but we were thrilled with our apartment at Cielito Lindo, which, roughly translated, means 'cute little heaven'. It was well named. We had a very spacious apartment with kitchen, monster double bed (6'5" wide, more "romping space!"), nice en suite, two big paddle fans, fridge and doors opening onto a private patio with a comfy seating area separated from the nice-sized swimming pool by potted plants. Bougainvillea and an unknown blue flowering climber covered the high wall and fencing at the back of the pool where we saw tiny hummingbirds sipping nectar. For £25 a night we didn't feel hard done by.

Quietly situated, the place was just a two-minute stroll to a parade of shops and restaurants known as Rinconada, and all round town we discovered that there were always taxis about who would take you anywhere in Puerto Escondido, which means 'hidden port', for 30 pesos, which is just over a quid.

The first thing we noticed was how much hotter this place was than anywhere else we'd been in Mexico. If you look at the map it is just about as far south as you can go in the country; in fact, it's further south than most parts of Guatemala. Much as we like walking, the taxis became an important part of our time at the resort. The heat and humidity from 11am to 4pm are not to be trifled with and the distances are considerable, so it just made sense to grab a cab and avoid heatstroke.

On our first morning there we took a cab to the town market, which was a huge affair with many stalls selling beautifully arranged fruit and veg, some familiar and some exotic. There was a fish section too, plus meat and cheese, so after walking all the way around Jilly homed in on the best-looking stall and, armed with her 'bags for life' all the way from Asda, proceeded to fill them up with everything she felt we needed for a week's self-catering. Staggering under this load, we lurched off to the cheese stall to sample some of their wares and finally to a place that boasted Pollos Rancheros, where they boned, flattened and roasted farm chickens. We bought a whole one for very little money. In fact, the whole exercise, including taxi fares and enough food to feed an army, only cost about £13. It also meant that I didn't have to go to the gym that day, having had a damn good workout.

Within walking distance we discovered two little horseshoe-shaped coves, both with soft, clean sand, palm trees and shady restaurants where you could make use of sun beds all day if you bought a drink or a snack. Sheltered from the massive Pacific rollers by high cliffs, these coves offered clear, relatively calm water with pretty good snorkelling, so we spent some happy hours there watching the Mexican families enjoying themselves. The only snag was that there were loads of steps down to the beach. On the rocks flanking one cove we saw a dad and his young son fishing. The little lad tried extra hard to cast and lost his balance in the process, so into the drink he went! He bobbed up straight away, still clutching his fishing rod, which his dad took from him first before helping the kid out of the water. Like us, the kid thought it was hilarious and it was good to see that dad had got his priorities right.

The main beach, though, was Playa Principal, which started off as a sheltered cove where the fishermen moored their boats, but as it extended along the coast it became more and more exposed to the Pacific rollers. After about a mile those rollers broke with explosive force on Playa Zicatela, which apparently is rated as the third best surfing beach in the world.

One morning we took a cab to Playa Principal, where we booked a boat fishing trip with Antonio for the next day, then paddled our way along the shore until we got to Zicatela, where we sat ourselves down to watch the surfing action. And what a show it was, with some brilliant athletes strutting their stuff and lots getting horribly wiped out as the huge waves broke in a great wall of thunderous spray. Somehow, they always seemed to emerge unscathed and paddled out to try again. Sitting in the hot sun watching this free show unfold absorbed us for ages, but then it was beer 'o'clock and light refreshments under a parasol were called for.

The boat trip at dawn the next morning started off with a bit of a surprise. We'd made it clear to the boatman that the price agreed was just for Jilly and me, but a young French-Canadian couple turned up as well. Antonio told me in a stage whisper that he'd actually agreed a higher price with them for an extra 90 minutes, but he wouldn't charge us any extra providing we didn't tell them what we'd agreed, so off we set into the rising sun.

It worked out quite well as it happened. The chap wanted to fish but his lady was shattered after a horrendous bus journey from Oaxaca the day before, so she ended up dozing whilst he and I chatted and fished. Unfortunately, we caught nothing at all in nearly five hours, but we did see literally hundreds of turtles and many dolphins, too. We gathered that the turtles were massing in readiness for storming the beaches that night for their annual egg laying. The sea was calm and all in all it was most pleasant – apart from the lack of fish.

After hearing about the French-Canadians' ghastly bus journey, we decided to abandon our original plan to take the eight-hour bus to Oaxaca, which was our next stop, and splash out yet again on the 35-minute flight. I popped into a travel agent's to get it booked. There was a lot of phoning to and fro and plenty of rapid tapping of computer keys, and after what seemed ages, she told me that there was only one seat left on the one plane a day that did the trip. Seeing my dismay, she brightly suggested that it was not a problem as my wife could follow the next day. My emphatic "No!" resulted in yet more key tapping and phone calls at the prospect of losing business, and after another half hour she announced triumphantly that she'd managed to find two seats on the day we wanted. Did she bump some poor single traveller, so she could sell two tickets instead? We'll never know.

Foolishly I'd made the big mistake of boasting to someone back in England that we'd never had a tummy problem in Mexico. Therefore, it followed that halfway through our week in Puerto Escondido Montezuma's Revenge struck us both on the same day. Not severe, just a bit of a nuisance, so we had a day off and stayed at our cute little heaven all day, and next day all was well again.

We scrambled down a sandy, steep path down the cliff to a sheltered bay where I tried fishing off the beach with a spinner. Every few minutes we'd walk a bit further along a seemingly endless beach with not a scrap of rubbish to be seen. Sadly, the fish were in equally short supply, so we stopped and walked up the beach to a hotel restaurant for a well-deserved beer, only to find that it was the day of the election of the new mayor and no alcohol was to be sold. I'm sure there's some logic to it somewhere, but it escapes me for the moment. Anyway, we went to the place next door where they had no such scruples and a nasty incident was avoided.

That evening we found a lovely restaurant perched on the cliff top above one of the little coves and we enjoyed a marvellous dinner as we watched the sun set behind the Pacific. Whilst the sunset was good, and some of the Americans actually applauded it (!!) it wasn't spectacular. However, within ten minutes of the sun disappearing the sky started to colour up again and within half an hour it was worthy of applause as the western sky glowed crimson.

Being gluttons for punishment we'd booked another four hours' fishing the next day, but this time we felt sure to succeed as our Capitan was called Jesus. Sure enough, shortly after setting off I had a violent take but then it all went slack as some toothy swine sliced through the line. Jesus tried really hard to find fish, and at one point deliberately joined a big pod of spinner dolphins in the hope that they were chasing tuna. Although that ploy didn't work, we were treated to the most amazing display of marine acrobatics as the dolphins played all around us, actually banging into the boat and living up to their name as they leapt spinning out of the ocean. We also saw many manta rays leaping as well. Useless information: manta is Spanish for blanket, hence the name. Compared to the previous trip there were very few turtles, most of them having done their laying. Jesus hooked a swordfish very briefly but it got away, and although he very kindly gave us another hour in the hope of breaking our duck it was not to be.

The boatmen have an interesting trick when they've finished with their boats for the day. Two or three of their mates try and keep people away from the patch of sand at the top of the beach where they intend to park the boat. Then, at a given signal, the captain gives the twin engines maximum power and charges straight for the beach. As the boat leaves the water the assistants drop long sticks in its path so the boat shoots straight up the beach to the parking spot. It's all very dramatic!

Suddenly, or so it seemed, our week's stay was over. We had to be at the airport two hours before our 8am flight, so we took a taxi and arrived at the airport by 5.50. However, the gates were locked and guarded by two security men. Our driver explained that they didn't open until 6, another 10 minutes, so I thought I'd save time by paying him at that point. Well, he thought I was saying don't bother to wait, we'll walk the rest of the way, so the next thing we knew our luggage was out of the cab and he was off. The guards let us through a side gate and it was only then that we realised we had a considerable distance to go up a fair old gradient, towing our cases.

When we got to the departures building the Aerotucan desk was unmanned and it wasn't until another half hour had passed that a sleepy-looking bod rolled up and checked us in. Rant number three: why the bloody hell do they tell you to be there two hours before your flight if they can't be bothered to turn up?

Another surprise awaited us when we saw our plane, but that's a tale for another day.

Buskers, Infinity Pools
and Monty Don

For years we've heard fellow travellers extolling the virtues of 'Wahaka', but every time we got home and I tried to look it up I just couldn't find anything about it – until last year I finally twigged that Oaxaca is not spelt with a 'W'. Duh!

The plane to Oaxaca turned out to be a single propeller 12-seater with headroom inside of about four feet. Just to make it interesting, a truly enormous man had parked himself on the first seat as you got in, which meant he was almost blocking the already very narrow aisle. We all had to bend double, carrying our hand luggage, and somehow push past this obstacle to get to our seats. We were sitting one seat away from the pilot, with no separation between him and the passengers. We could see all his instruments – including a satnav thingy so we could track where we were.

We set off down the runway right on time, gently lifted off and as we gradually gained height the pilot executed a slow turn over the town and out to sea, which gave us a stunning view of the two little coves. He then headed back over land in a northerly direction, all the time gaining altitude so that by the time we were over the mountain range we were about a thousand feet above the peaks. We were so close to the tops of the mountains that not only could we see that they were forested but we could make out each individual tree. I noticed that quite a few needed pruning.

After 20 minutes the mountains were replaced by a fertile valley heavily used for agriculture, and our plane gradually lost altitude as we approached Oaxaca airport. The landing, exactly 35 minutes after take-off, was so smooth it didn't even wake the co-pilot, who had been snoring his head off all the way! It was the most relaxing plane journey we've ever had (once we managed to get to our seats).

Whilst I waited for our bags, I watched Jilly saunter gracefully into the gents', but I was too far away to call out. It didn't seem to faze her, but then not much does.

A quick ride in a colectivo for £3 each took us directly to our next home, which was a self-catering apartment with a rooftop patio giving fabulous views over the city of trees and the surrounding mountains, for Oaxaca is set in a highland valley. The apartment was very modern, with marble tiled en suite, kitchen with induction hobs (we're not too sure what they are but they seem to cook in a weird sort of way) and two flat screen TVs, one in the bedroom and one in the open plan living area. There was a huge range of CDs and DVDs as well as a thousand Mexican TV channels. Amongst these gems we found the complete collection of Friends in English, so we didn't bother too much with the rest, especially as it took me several hours to figure out how to get the buggers to play.

Our place was within 15 minutes' walk of the centre, or zocalo, which is an enormous square surrounded by beautiful colonial buildings, some converted to restaurants with open air tables and chairs under parasols, and a huge, impressive cathedral which, typically, has been built and re-built several times since the 16th century thanks to earthquakes. In the middle of the zocalo there is a raised bandstand, which is often used for that purpose, and lots of big, ancient shade trees.

If you sit at one of the restaurants you can watch an amazing floor show of passers-by. The indigenous native people – and I will risk being non-politically correct by referring to them as Indians from now on, for the sake of brevity – tend to be tiny people. Even sitting down, I am taller than most of the women and many of the men. They wear regional costumes and they are mostly there to sell their wares – and they make a LOT of stuff. This means that every few seconds an Indian lady will approach you clutching carvings, paintings, carved combs, bracelets, shawls, rugs, hats and lots of things that we couldn't even recognise. Not all together, you understand; different ladies carry different products, of course. A shake of the head or a simple "No gracias" is enough to send them on their way, so it is all very gentle and non-threatening, but there ain't 'alf a lot of 'em! Then there are the buskers. Single or in groups, singers, guitarists, xylophonists, drummers, panpipers, trumpeters, saxophonists, you name it. Some are great, some we would happily pay to shut up, but again they're never pushy.

One night there was a live band with lots of people ballroom dancing under the stars, which was lovely to see, everybody so happy and relaxed. Some days were magic shows or audience participation games. There was always some free entertainment, so we spent a lot of time there.

One reason for visiting the city was to visit the oldest mega civilisation in the Americas, Monte Alban (or Monty Don, as Jilly calls it). Oaxaca is 1770 metres high, but Monte Alban is located way above that on top of a mountain overlooking the 'modern' city. The place was huge, with much climbing of steep steps to make the most of the magnificent views. This was the capital of the Zapotec empire that ruled this part of the Americas from 500BC until about 800AD, acting as the major power between the Mayans and the Teotihuacan. The air's a bit thin at this altitude, so it was hard work hiking around in the heat and we spent the afternoon slobbing on our nice rooftop in the company of the occasional hummingbird. We often hear parrots but never see them. Mind you, sometimes we hear cattle lowing, but it wasn't until we'd been there for several days that we realised it was an amplified recording attached to the truck of a mobile butcher! You can't trust anyone!

On Sunday we had a wonderful walk to the other side of the city where the original stone viaduct built by the conquistadores in the 16th century to bring in water from the mountains is still intact – or chunks of it, anyway. The streets were partly pedestrianised, and we found some cute little cobbled lanes made even prettier by the many flowering shrubs and trees here. Bougainvillea does very well but there is also a tall tree that's absolutely smothered in bright yellow flowers, almost like our laburnum; we have christened it 'el laburno', which seems more appropriate here.

Under a clear blue sky and in a lovely

temperature, our walk led us to one of the principal churches in Oaxaca where the patron saint of the city stands over the nave in effigy form, wearing a crown made of five pounds of solid gold and inlaid with five hundred diamonds. The church was packed so there was no chance of us nicking anything. Outside the church was a square lined with what we thought were cafes but when we asked for tea, they explained that they were all ice cream parlours. However, we found one daring soul who offered cakes instead. We had one of their pastry cornets stuffed with custard – scrumptious!

Then our walk took us back to the zocalo where, to our amazement, there was a 50-piece orchestra playing classical music under the shade of the big trees. Brilliant!

A little later in the day the sound of a brass band heralded a protest march in the zocalo against rising fuel prices, with the band leading hundreds of people carrying placards, and a line of many tuc-tucs beeping their horns. You never knew what was going to turn up next.

We forked out a quid each for an hour-long colectivo ride to one of the outlying towns, Ocotlan, where, once a week, they have a huge Indian market. We wandered for hours among awnings under which thousands of Indians were selling an absolute kaleidoscope of produce. There were people walking about with live turkeys, chickens, ducks and goats on leads; mountains of fruit and veg, some familiar, mostly not; clothes and hats; and fantastic blacksmith products from machetes to, unbelievably, iron ploughshares. One stall was even selling full size wooden ploughs, which we've only ever seen in museums, but here they still manufacture and use them. Then there were areas where cooking and eating was going on, and we courageously had some shredded beef tacos with some sort of greens. The noise, sights and smells were intoxicating: troubadours competing with vendors shouting and the tiny people trying to make themselves heard over the bedlam. Eventually we got spat out for a breather and found a quiet cafe for a beer and a tea, before diving back in for more entertainment. We bought a couple of little presents for loved ones and then caught the bus back to Oaxaca. The whole marvellous day, including transport, lunch, presents and refreshments, cost £6 for the two of us. Oh no, we don't skimp!

On our last day we paid £10 each for an all-day tour, starting in a village where they have one of the biggest trees in the world, some kind of cypress allegedly over 2000 years old. It may not be anything like as tall as a giant redwood, but it is enormously fat and quite a sight. The journey continued to a place where they made wool and used natural products to dye it, such as cochineal, and they demonstrated how each colour was produced. Much as I love the science of wool dyeing, I much preferred the next item on the agenda – a visit to a mezcal manufacturer with the obligatory tasting of various vintages. We actually bought some this time. A tasty buffet lunch was next, and finally a long drive high into the dramatic mountain scenery took us to a semi-petrified waterfall where some went swimming in what must be the highest infinity pool in the world, with just a thin lip between bathers and a sheer drop to, naturally, infinity.

When we arrived back at the apartment Jilly commented, "Who's stolen our days?" Once again, it was time to move on.

School Projects, Resident Dogs and Sacred Cola

Our fourth and final domestic flight saw us on a two-propeller plane with proper headroom and a toilet, plus the arrival of a trolley of soft drinks halfway through the 70-minute flight. We were heading to the highland town of San Cristobal de las Casas, but the plane only took us as far as Tuxtla Gutierrez (easy for you to say), which is the nearest airport. There we had a cup of tea and a cake while we waited for a smart, modern minibus to drive us for another hour up a new toll road, which climbed higher and higher for the whole journey through some stunning mountain scenery until it arrived at

San Cris, as it shall be named from now on. This town is about as high as Mexico City but is obviously much smaller and first impressions were that it was bursting with charm. There's a hint of Alpine about it, with pantile roofs and overhanging eaves plus some magnificent churches.

This town gets cold at night (seven degrees) and our next home was a character cottage complete with open fire to keep us warm. Usually there are no nasty surprises when we arrive at a new place, but this one wasn't quite what we expected. On paper, it had everything it advertised on Airbnb: en suite, kitchen, etcetera etcetera. However, the kitchen was separated from the cottage by a couple of outside doors and the en suite was downstairs whereas the bedroom was upstairs. Also, the journey from bedroom to bathroom involved bending double to avoid 'character' beams and negotiating a slippery, spiral staircase with no handrail and, as if it were needed, some more brain-smashing low beams. Still, at £19 a night, a little concussion is acceptable collateral damage.

Being a gentleman of a certain age I find it necessary to visit the bathroom at least a thousand times a night, so this situation presented an interesting challenge. Clearly, lateral thinking was called for. We bought a large bottle of drinking water and drank the contents, and the container then lived in the bedroom and was known as the 'first floor en suite'. Problem solved.

The cottage is set in a beautifully planted garden enclosed by high walls. A yellow rose-like climber scrambles up the outside walls and there is bougainvillea, too, with ground cover provided by magnificent arum lilies interspersed with variegated foliage plants and ferns. Towering over this lot is a flame tree which is a magnet for hummingbirds. There was a long-haired old cat, whose sole ambition seemed to be to get into our cottage, and a big black Labrador, who was very friendly. Also peering in at us was a turkey in a pen, which could be a little disconcerting but made us giggle when he gobbled!

Ako, the Labrador, had a habit of scratching his back, and it so happens that the dwarf retaining wall surrounding our patio was exactly the right height for him, so he would walk alongside the wall, leaning in at an angle, with an expression of ecstasy on his face. The only problem was there were lines of agapanthus planted on the edge of the wall, with their leaves overhanging, and every time the dog rubbed along the wall, he left a trail of smashed leaves. He didn't give a hoot.

We spent the first day exploring the town, with some of the steeper hills making us a little breathless thanks to the altitude. Our aimless wandering took us to yet another wonderful market bustling with mini Indians in ever more exotic outfits. Up until now it had only been the women who wore the ethnic gear, with the blokes generally dressed like pocket-sized cowboys in jeans and straw Stetsons, but here we saw some of the men in tribal clothing, too. I'd read that the Indians in this area can get upset if you photograph them, so I tried to be discreet about it. However, one lady gave me a telling off, so we did need to be careful.

One day we hiked for 20 minutes to a place devoted to the study and protection of the indigenous tribes in the area. We gathered that there are over 30 Mayan tribes, each speaking a different dialect. This place was a huge, rambling hacienda-type place that was bought by a Danish/Dutch couple who'd been studying the Indians since the 1920s and wanted a base/museum for their enterprise. We wanted to learn more about it as we planned to go to one of the principal ethnic villages in the area later that day.

Sure enough, later found us on a colectivo stuffed to the gills with mini Indians and two huge gringos (us!) as the driver hurtled up a winding mountain road to the town of San Juan Chamula. Half an hour later we arrived in the big main square of the village, which was dominated by the large white Templo San Juan. We paid a few pesos and went in to witness one of the weirdest places we'd ever seen. Of course, photography was strictly forbidden, so the description will have to suffice.

The title gives a slight clue that this is not your

normal church. It is, in fact, a chunk of Christianity coupled with the ancient ethnic religions. As we entered, we were first aware of the smell of incense and the sight of literally thousands of flickering candles, some on the marble floor and others on low tables or shelves. The floor was covered in pine needles and, as our eyes became accustomed to the gloom, we could see family groups setting out their candles before lighting them and kneeling or prostrating themselves in prayer, but with offerings such as bottles of Coke just to make things interesting. We gather that they also sacrifice chickens, and although we heard one, we were spared that particular sight. All around the inside of the temple, in glass cases, were labelled effigies of every saint imaginable. There were crosses to be seen, and indeed the effigy of Jesus was a little bigger than the others and also had fairy lights to indicate his greater importance, but it was certainly like no church we'd ever been to. We were a bit concerned about fire hazards. The Indian ladies here, no doubt because of the high altitude, wear skirts of sheep wool, so they're very thick and hairy (the skirts, not the women) and there is this layer of highly inflammable pine needles on the floor, so when you add candles to the mix – well, Health & Safety wouldn't be too impressed, that's for sure.

It seemed that every time we tried to get into one of the big old churches here they were firmly closed for siesta, so one morning we set off to get stuck in before lunch time. Sure enough, we'd done two churches, a cathedral and a museum before noon, with the last church up a flight of something like 100 steep steps, but the reward at the top was a fabulous view of the town and a very pretty church. Coming down was easy, although a zip line would have been more fun, and at the bottom we found the Fanny Cafe – which seemed like a suitable reward for all the effort but sadly was just the name of the owner.

Our host at the cottage was a hippy chap, half Mexican and half American, and his daughter had her second birthday while we were there, so during our hikes we found a wonderful sweet shop where you could choose from an absolute kaleidoscope of different sweets. Jilly chose one of each, which were duly weighed, and we parted with 50p for a big bagful which we later presented to the birthday girl.

Talking of hippies, if you're wondering where they've all gone this is the place. There are hippies from all over the world here, weaving mysterious objects which they try to sell in between busking (badly, for the most part). One day Jilly suddenly stopped walking and when I asked her what the problem was, she explained that she'd got downwind of a particularly fragrant character and was waiting for him to move away. Hose 'em down, I say, or put them to work building the Trump Wall...

On our last day here we decided to hike to one of

the churches that's built way up on hills overlooking the city. My navigation went a bit wrong and we somehow ended up at an amber museum. It seems that the state of Chiapas, where we were, is one of the principal places in the world for mining amber, and there was an excellent display with equally good text in English – unlike most museums in Mexico, where it is usually either all in Spanish or there is an awful English translation. So now we know how to tell real amber from fake.

It was the hottest day since we've been here, so inevitably we walked around for ages trying to get our bearings in the hot sun before finally arriving at the base of the steps leading to the church at 12:35pm. Mad dogs and Englishmen, etcetera. Still, there were only 290 of them (steps, not Englishmen) so we took it in easy stages and finally made it to a fairly nondescript church with super views.

Halfway up the steps a bunch of local kids swooped on us with pencils and paper, saying they were on a school project. "What is your name? What country? How old are you?" they asked us. The last question was, "How much would you like to donate?" Well, we could see from the previous entries that they'd cunningly added at least a couple of zeros to previous gringos' responses (500 pesos instead of 5), so we paid them 10 for their cheek and I gave them a packet of English chewing gum as well. I expect the stairs are sticky now.

It was all downhill from there on, of course, and we had a lazy lunch whilst trying in vain to take sneaky photos of passing hippies and Indians. In the end we cheated and negotiated a deal with a couple of Indian ladies whereby we paid them 20 pesos in return for a pic.

On our last night we paid our second visit to an absolutely brilliant restaurant only 200 yards from our cottage. We'd passed it several times thinking it was just another vegetarian hippy breakfast place, but then discovered that there was a full-blown Italian restaurant hidden inside, owned by a stereotypical Neapolitan complete with beard, white chef's tunic, and ultra-dramatic Italian accent and body language. Having been there only once before, he came close to tears of emotion when he saw us for the second time. He gave Jilly a big hug and, had she not been present, would probably have shagged me there and then. A narrow escape indeed. Our meal was memorable, and it worked out at £12 each, including wine.

And so tomorrow morning we jump on the bus down the mountain to the steamy jungle, and yet another exciting adventure.

Bug Spray, Tombs
and All-inclusive Zoos

Perhaps the most comfortable bus in the world awaited us next morning for our journey down the mountains to the town of Palenque. The bus had the softest, biggest reclining armchairs instead of seats, with loads of leg room, and as is usual in the land of manana we set off dead on time. There was some uncertainty about exactly how long the journey would take, though. I thought the lady at the bus station who sold me the tickets said seven hours, but everything I'd read said five, so we hoped that something had gone amiss with the translation.

I do like my maps, but according to mine – and

according to the sun – we were actually going in the opposite direction to Palenque. I had a moment of panic but then remembered that the bus had Palenque clearly visible on the front, and our tickets showed Palenque as the destination, too, so what on earth was going on? I queried this with another gringo who confirmed that we were on the right bus but they weren't using the direct route at the moment because there was "a little civil war going on" and the road was blockaded by protesters.

The magic bus took us down the mountains alright, on a superbly engineered road with amazing views, but they were familiar views. In fact, we were heading back to Tuxtla Gutierrez where we'd flown on our way to San Cris, and we were indeed going in the opposite direction to our destination. I checked my crude little map and tried to work out how we could get to Palenque, but the only route I could see took us a vastly roundabout way, which surely couldn't be right.

Well, it was! The bus took us on a huge, circular route through Tuxtla Gutierrez, then north all the way into the state of Tobasco and the city of Villahermosa, up a dreadful potholed winding road through the thick jungle where a big bus like ours should never have ventured, then on to flat, fertile land and a dead straight super highway, along a stretch of unmade road where all the vegetation was covered in a thick layer of white dust from the traffic, and through cattle country with big fields dotted with shade trees, where the cattle dozed and cowboys with white Stetsons rode their horses. Actually, Jilly saw two cowboys gallop into a petrol station, unlikely though it may seem. There was a brief pit stop for a snack and a drink, and then onward, ever onward until just over eight hours later we drew into Palenque bus station. Now I know why we kept cheating and taking those nice little flights instead of the bus, no matter how luxurious it may be! But having said all that, we did see a lot of Mexico that we hadn't bargained on, including some fascinating and varied countryside, and I did have a couple of nice dozes, so it wasn't all bad.

Our new home was a hotel right across the road from the bus station. It was perfectly adequate, with aircon, en suite, two double beds and a swimming pool, which we were going to need because it seems ferociously hot here compared to our last two hilly homes. It's coming to something when your sandals are too hot, but that's the situation here. Scorchio!

We found a nice restaurant close by our hotel for dinner, with a fountain providing a soothing background sound. We were waiting for our meal to be cooked when the waiter suddenly burst into a run towards the fountain and presumably switched something off, but too late because water started pouring over the edge of the water feature heading downhill, as water tends to do, and straight for our table! We moved to the next one and then watched the waiter dash back to the kitchen, emerging seconds later with a silver champagne bucket which he filled from the offending water feature, rushed back a few yards and emptied onto a needy potted plant. This performance was repeated half a dozen times until the deluge was averted and he could resume life at slow speed. More free entertainment, but we resisted the urge to applaud.

A 20-peso colectivo took us to the raisin d'etre for our being here, the lost Mayan city of Palenque. Over the years we've visited all the major ruins except this one, and we're so glad we made the effort because it is definitely one of our favourites. The ancients built this city where the huge plain of Yucatan meets the first hills of Chiapas, and now this stunning place emerges from the jungle, with parrots flying past and a crystal-clear stream with waterfalls giving some clue as to how wonderful it must have been in its heyday. Many of the buildings are substantially intact, complete with painted stucco and carvings, and it is possible to walk inside some of the temples within high, corbelled ceilings. You can even visit the Temple of Inscriptions, where archaeologists found the intact engraved sarcophagus of the big cheese, Pakal the Great, complete with jade face mask and lots of bling.

We wandered round for hours in the hot and humid jungle, marvelling at all the stunning architecture as it emerged from the forest, the haunting sound of howler monkeys giving it even more atmosphere. The only negative was a crowd of very loud German tourists with an even louder guide. People who shout in whatever language in places like this should be exterminated in my view, but then I always had liberal tendencies.

Finally it was time to visit the museum where the principal finds were to be seen, but we'd forgotten it was a Monday which meant that it was bloody closed! We planned to go back in a couple of days to try again, but meanwhile we had a major trip organised next day, which meant a 4.30 alarm. What kind of holiday is this?

Our full day tour started with a comfortable minibus picking us up in the dark at 6am and we set off for a long drive south east. The break of dawn revealed that we were travelling along a broad valley with the mist-enshrouded hills of Mexico on one side and Guatemala on the other. After an hour and a half we stopped for a buffet breakfast of scrambled eggs and bacon, refried beans, rice, bread, fruit and tea or coffee, all excellent.

We passed little villages where dogs dozed on the roadside, pigs on leads grazed, chickens, ducks and turkeys roamed free and cowboys trotted along, looking for another petrol station presumably.

Another hour or so took us to the bank of a mighty fast-flowing river which is the border with

Guatemala, and there we hopped onto a narrow wooden boat with a thatched roof and a 60hp Mercury engine for a half hour ride downstream, avoiding the rapids as the river raced past the jungle. Then we gently beached onto soft sand and our guide led us up steep steps into the jungle to explore yet another lost Mayan city (Why were they so careless?) tucked away in this inaccessible site. In fact, the Spanish conquerors missed this one altogether, and it was only discovered by a French archaeologist relatively recently. As a result, much of it is in very good nick and our guide took us into internal passages, with bats dozing on the ceiling and howler monkeys roaring away to provide exotic background effects. In fact, a troupe of monkeys were clearly visible very close by and totally drowned the guide's voice with their calling.

When we spotted the howler monkey gang I, like all the others, immediately concentrated on trying to get photos of them, and stepped forward to get a closer view ... only to realise I was falling into a three-foot deep pit! Somehow, I managed to land upright, but my momentum carried me forward at such speed that I was in danger of crashing into the opposite wall. By some miracle I managed to leap up onto level ground again like a pronking gazelle (well, not quite as graceful), still with the iPad clutched before me and hoping that everyone else had been too preoccupied to witness this amazing feat! I looked back at the pit thinking I might have grounds for litigation as they hadn't fenced it off, but then noticed there was a big sign forbidding people to enter it because in the centre was an enormous ancient carved stone pillar, which I'd somehow avoided during my acrobatics. Don't tell anyone.

Our tour of this place took over two hours, and then it was back on the boat for another fairly hairy ride up the 200-feet wide river, pausing only when we spotted a largish crocodile basking on a sand bank and then sliding into the river when he spotted us. We passed Guatemalan ladies standing in the shallows washing clothes before we got back to the minibus and a short drive to a roadside restaurant for a delicious lunch.

Another hour's drive took us to the last venue, which was a smaller Mayan site, again in the jungle, notable for three rooms with remarkably intact brightly painted frescoes showing scenes from this city's glory days. By this time the sun was nearly over the horizon and our long drive back to Palenque was smooth enough. This very full and enjoyable day only cost £32 each including meals, transport by road and river, entrance fees and national park fees. Bargain!

That night we had dinner in a restaurant owned by a hippy German where they cooked a very good arrachera steak with salad. There was a bottle of vinaigrette on our table, which Jilly used on her salad. But then the German owner approached offering her what she assumed was a bottle of dressing. She explained she'd already used the dressing on the table. "Nein," he said, waving his bottle in the air, "zis is bug spray in case you need it!" We burst out laughing, and I joked that we English always used vinaigrette to keep the bugs off, but he didn't get it, and walked away with a puzzled look on his face.

The next day was supposed to be a day off, except for a leisurely trip to the museum we'd missed because it was closed. However, after some debate we decided to call first at an 'eco park' on the way which purported to look after rescued wildlife until they could be returned to the jungle. It sounded like a zoo to us – and we're not too keen on that concept, having seen some shockers on our travels – but good reviews on Google persuaded us to go, and what a treat it turned out to be.

We walked for three hours along a well-built broad path that meandered through beautiful planting that merged into the surrounding jungle. Around every bend was a surprise: an island surrounded by water, where monkeys amused us with their acrobatics; lakes with enormous crocodiles; pools where pink flamingos waded whilst waterfalls played behind them; tapirs, ocelots, jaguars (not the four wheeled variety) and black panthers; and aviaries you could walk through, full of parrots and love birds, scarlet macaws screeching as they flew overhead, and all the time exotic birdsong, sometimes deafening, but the birds themselves concealed in the dense foliage. The highlight of this visit was to a lake where there were at least four manatees that came to the bank when called and we were allowed to feed them a selection of chopped fruit by hand. These huge, trusting mammals were so gentle and it was a unique experience for us. Our conclusion was that all these creatures were living the life of Reilly in an all-inclusive resort, or so it seemed to us. Nothing like a zoo.

Hundreds of photos later we left this garden of Eden and, after a short walk, found a fabulous thatched roof restaurant, with open sides to give some welcome ventilation on another baking hot day, and lovely planting, where we shared a club sandwich and drinks. Chatting to the waiter in my Spanglish, I learned that the small lake in the grounds contained fish. Next thing, we were standing on a wooden bridge spanning the lake, feeding bread to the carp below. We never actually saw them; the water was like pea soup (visually, before you ask. I wasn't about to taste it!) but the fish devoured the bread once they'd groped their way to it.

Eventually we made our way to the 'ruinas' again and paid once more in order to see the museum, but as the ticket included the ruins we couldn't resist taking a second, abbreviated trip round this splendid site before finally viewing the wonderful finds within the museum – including the huge stone sarcophagus. However, the jade mask that covered the king's face in death was nowhere to be seen. When I asked about it, they told me it was in a museum in Mexico City. Doh!

When we totted it up, we realised that we had been walking, including hundreds of steps, for a total of at least six hours. Some day off, but thoroughly enjoyable.

And so we're now at the end of our three days in the town of Palenque, and tomorrow morning we set off for the Gulf of Mexico. I don't suppose much will happen there, but you never know...

Prawns, Stakes and Clifftop Battlements

The plan was a good one. Jilly would go and pack on our last evening in Palenque whilst I sat in a nearby bar and sipped a Cuba Libre whilst finishing off our 'postcard', so we could send it off before we left. The sun was low and the temperature was perfect – as was the Cuba Libre – and I reflected on how the spirit measures with these Mexican cocktails seem so generous but somehow don't have the same effect as back in England. Maybe here we sweat out the alcohol, or they water it down – who knows? But it was all very pleasant, so I ordered a refill and pressed on with the email until it was done, paid the modest bill and walked back to the room.

A few moments later there was a knock on the door and there, to my surprise, was the waiter from the bar clutching my hat. I thanked him sincerely, as it had taken me 30 years to find one that fitted me. But then he showed me the bill. It was for 170 pesos, but I'd misread it and only left 140 on the table. Red-faced, I coughed up the rest plus a generous tip and started to revise my opinion of Mexican cocktails whilst Jilly gave me 'the look'.

A six-hour bus journey next day took us to the city of Campeche on the Gulf of Mexico. This is a most beautiful colonial city, a UNESCO World Heritage Site, with well-restored buildings brightly painted in different shades, set within the ancient city walls, built to defend the town against frequent attacks by pirates (mostly British, I'm proud to say) in the 17th and 18th centuries. We'd been here before and so enjoyed it we thought we'd just break the journey for another couple of days.

Imagine our surprise when, as we were walking along following the city walls and the various museums set into them, we came across the very same German hippy who'd offered us the bug spray! It seems his daughter was entered in a roller skate competition in Merida and his wife had relatives in Campeche, so they'd stopped off to visit. What are the chances, eh?

We took a 35-peso taxi to one of the two 18th

century forts up on the high hill overlooking both sea and city. I love this period for its architecture, and this place doubles the enjoyment with a very interesting museum set into the ground floor rooms plus splendid views from the battlements. There is a cunning twisted entrance so invaders couldn't see the horrors waiting for them until it was too late. Then, if they survived that, there's a deep moat which, in the old days, was full of sharpened stakes below a drawbridge. Lovely!

From the fort, we walked about two miles down a steep and winding road to a fishing port on the estuary where they were selling fresh fish and mending their nets. Some American friends had kindly advised us of a cluster of seafood palapas along the malecon (promenade) and after another mile or so, in considerable heat, we came upon them and sat down for a well-deserved lunch of huge, beautifully cooked prawns and a couple of drinks as we took in the sea view.

Next day we caught the 6am luxury coach for a two-hour ride to the city of Merida as part one of a very long journey to Isla Holbox. In Merida we had a snack before taking another coach trip to Valladolid, getting there at midday and grabbing a taxi for a short ride to the main square of this colonial city, which we'd been to a couple of years ago. We had a relaxed lunch there in a courtyard garden next to the cathedral and, being a Sunday, we could just about hear pleasant singing coming from the church.

Lunch break over, it was time for another taxi back to the bus station – which was when things got interesting. The master plan was to take a second-class bus to Cancun but get off about halfway at the tiny hamlet of El Ideal (yes, really), which was the turn off for the road to Chiquila, the ferry port for our favourite island in all the world, Holbox. In El Ideal we hoped to get a taxi for the remaining journey, but it was all a bit on a wing and a prayer.

Well, it was at this point that things began to unravel. For the first time we experienced a Mexican bus that was late. The bus station was the worst we'd been to: normally they're immaculate, but this one was overcrowded and very hot, yet they didn't bother to switch on the aircon or the fans. The bellowed tannoy announcements were so distorted that the locals were having problems deciphering them, let alone the gringos.

When the bus finally turned up there was a bit of a scrum to get on, which we'd never experienced before in this country. The locals kept queue jumping but we stayed calm, knowing we had booked seats. Again, unusually, there was no one to put our bags in the hold so we had to do it ourselves, and by the time we boarded the coach all the seats were taken and the driver told us it was standing room only. I pointed out that we had seat reservations, but he said it was not possible to book seats on second-class buses. "So why do our tickets show seats 22 and 23?" I demanded. He just shrugged. When I explained to Jilly, she refused point blank to stand for the 90-minute journey, so we got off, retrieved our bags, spat in the hold, complained bitterly at the ticket office and stalked out of the bus station into the blazing sun. Actually, I think we were more blazing than the sun. Time for Plan B.

I flagged down a taxi and asked him how much to the port of Chiquila, but before he could reply another taxi driver appeared from nowhere and started a fierce argument with the first driver. I thought they were going to come to blows! It seems the aggressive second driver thought he had a divine right to our business as his cab was parked in a rank, although we couldn't see one. Anyway, anyone that aggressive was certainly not going to be driving us around so we agreed a price of £40 with the first driver and off we went for a fast but relaxed two-hour journey to the ferry. Half an hour on the sunny top deck of the boat and we were back on Isla Holbox, all set for a nice, relaxing break after all the 'hard work'. My lovely cousin Ali had emailed to ask when we were going to find a beach and relax. Maybe the time had come?

The following day found us standing knee deep in clear, warm water, admiring the ever-changing colours of the sea and the gently swaying palms. The sun was hot on our backs and we had two whole weeks to look forward to with no long journeys. We both had a drink in hand and all was right with the world. "Aren't we lucky?" I said. Actually, I think I was luckier than Jilly because I had a margarita and she just had tea, but she didn't argue.

Chorus Girls, Fort Knox
and Noisy Neighbours

Holbox is Mayan for 'black hole', which is a little odd on the face of it, because this glorified sand bar is anything but. It's a long, narrow island in the Gulf of Mexico stretching almost up to where the Gulf meets the Caribbean, but only the relatively small area on the western tip is inhabited. A river divides the two sections near the aptly named Mosquito Point and it's a protected wildlife zone east of the river. In fact, the river just allows water to flow from the Gulf into the lagoon between the island and the mainland, so it's not a proper river, but we're told that there are crocodiles in it.

Sand is the name of the game here: a white sandy beach runs the whole length of the Gulf side for miles and miles. The roads are all made of the same stuff too, so sand inevitably gets trodden into everywhere. It even comes to bed with you on your feet, but you get used to it.

This is our third stay on the island; we just love it here. Some say there's not a lot to do but we don't find that. We love the long beach walks in the hot sun, splashing through the clear water in the shallows to keep cool, admiring the ever-changing colours of the sea, laughing at the gangs of razorbills all perched on the same boat like a bunch of chorus girls about to burst into a routine, pelicans effortlessly gliding by with such grace until they spot fish and then plunge in with an ungainly splash, little sanderlings scuttling about on the water's edge always a split second away from being swamped by the next wave, big sea eagles flapping by and, above them, the ever-watchful frigate birds, just waiting for a chance to rob some seagull of a meal but never landing in the water as they can't swim.

We love the fishing trips, too, from the beach at Cocoa Point and from the rickety wooden pier with the occasional deck board missing, just to make life interesting. And then there's the odd expensive treat of a boat trip with the prospect of something huge and an almost guaranteed ceviche or fresh fish dinner to follow.

The little town is a maze of sandy streets with little or nothing in the way of traffic control but there are hardly any proper vehicles here, just the occasional delivery pick up van. Pretty well every other vehicle is a golf cart, along with the odd motorbike, so people and golf carts weave in and out amongst each other with no one really having priority as far as we can see. Somehow it seems to work. There are shops and restaurants and bars and a town square. The only thing lacking is a reliable ATM – there is one, but it is usually broken or out of cash and tourists often get caught out when they run out of money as very few businesses accept credit cards. We bring lots of cash with us, but then it's a worry about how to keep it safe. Last year we invested in a travel safe, which is basically a tin box with a combination lock on the end of a thick wire, the idea being you can loop the wire round a water pipe or a bed frame and hide it under towels or clothing. It's not Fort Knox but it's better than nothing.

Being an island, it's usually breezy but for our first two days there was no wind – the sea was flat calm – and of course this made it even hotter than the usual 84 degrees, or at least it seemed that way. I joked that it wouldn't last: "Two fine days and a thunderstorm!" so, naturally, there was a lot of rain that night. Next day the roads were transformed into mini lakes and there was a gale force wind, but at least it was dry and still very warm. We took our usual beach walk but this time it was like a hot Blackpool, if that's not a contradiction in terms. That, by the way, was the only rain we've had in the last six weeks.

The day after, things were back to normal weather-wise, with a refreshing breeze during the day, and the roads fairly quickly lost their puddles.

We tried an afternoon's fishing from the beach at Punta Coco, which is normally very productive, but there was so much stirred-up weed after the gale that the fish probably couldn't even see the lure! It was enjoyable anyway.

Incidentally, the Spanish for bait is carnada, but when I went to the fishing tackle shop and said "Carnada?" the chap said, "No, we only take cash." It took me a moment to realise that he thought I'd said card in English, as in credit card.

Another evening I got some sardines to use as bait off the pier and caught fish after fish – mostly catfish, which I hate catching as they have vicious venomous spines. Some locals were fishing and catching very little, so I asked if they wanted mine. Their eyes lit up and after that every time I caught one there was an eager amigo to unhook the fish so they could take it home for supper. It pleased me no end: the fish fight well on light tackle, so I had fun and the locals had supper.

Talking of fun, one reason for coming here at this

time of year was that it ties in with Carnival Week. At any time of day or night we come across gangs of locals, mostly women, dressed in various outfits, dancing and singing to live bands. All we have to do is follow the music and there they are, our free entertainment. They appear to be split into different age groups, with a bunch of older women dressed as Hawaiian girls in grass skirts and floral headdresses, but with inflatable 'fat' waistbands (although some don't actually need them as there are some wholesome lasses around!). Another younger group were dressed as Jamaicans, complete with dreadlocks and tea cosy hats, and of course their band played appropriate Bob Marley-type music.

We booked a boat trip and were supposed to meet our captain, Odin (who you've met before!) at 8am but by 8.30 he still hadn't shown up. Eventually we tracked down his dad who explained that Odin had had too much fiesta, a problem we've had before here. Nothing daunted, we found another, relatively sober captain who only wanted to catch sea trout, but we went with him and caught loads on little plastic lures although it was hard work standing up and casting for four hours. Then Jilly hooked a whopper on a whole sardine and between the two of us we boated the biggest fish of the day, a yellowtail jack of about six pounds. We took three of the trout with us, pausing only to fall into a beachside bar. Anxious to get the fish prepared and in the fridge as soon as possible, we didn't stay long and walked the rest of the way back to our apartment, where we greatly enjoyed our dinner of fresh sea trout and salad. We gave one of the trout to our American neighbour, Maureen, and in return she gave us some chocolate tarts, which rounded off the meal perfectly.

Our apartment is one of a block of three bungalows, each with spacious kitchen/diner, big bedroom and en suite, aircon plus a nice patio with table and chairs, shaded by palm trees. We stayed here last year and for £25 a night we think it's good value. However, one day four young Mexican blokes moved in next door and immediately started to party on their patio. Why not, we thought, in our liberal way, but by 10.30 that night I was thinking of lots of reasons why not as their music gradually cranked up – as did my blood pressure as their voices rose to keep pace with the decibels from the radio.

Finally I could stand it no more. I steeled myself to go out and face them, but fortunately Mr Reasonable stepped in and advised me to stay calm. Softly softly catches monkey, etcetera. I spent some time quietly preparing my Spanish phrases so I could gently but firmly reason with them in their own language. When suitably prepared, I opened the front door expecting to find the four amigos, but was instead confronted by at least eight, and they'd even had the cheek to nick our chairs! The noise was devastating, but I kept calm. Unfortunately, what came out of my mouth was not the carefully rehearsed, well-reasoned plea for peace and consideration but the very Anglo-Saxon bellow of "Oy!" And then, as it seemed to have some effect, an even louder "Oy!!!" accompanied by furious 'keep it down' gestures. The music and the shouting stopped dramatically. "Now they're going to kill me," I thought, and was all set to step back inside and bolt the door, but instead one of them apologised profusely. Much relieved and grateful to have survived both the cardiac arrest and the imagined machete attack, I wished them buenos noches and went back to bed, although it was some considerable time before my breathing got back to normal and I was able to sleep.

We're in our final week before this holiday ends, and other than the encounter with the neighbours our time here on Holbox has been very peaceful. But as ever, who knows what the next few days will hold?

Pufferfish, Manta Rays and Shell Dwellers

We've now been in Mexico for seven weeks and we've only had two mosquito bites each in all that time, which is pretty amazing – especially for Jilly, who appears to be particularly flavoursome to our little friends. We take anti-malaria pills once a week, which for some reason aren't sugar coated so they taste really awful. So awful that we call them death pills and try to swallow them as quickly as we possibly can.

Fishing off the rickety wooden dock first thing in a very strong wind I caught several big catfish and lots of pufferfish, which are a real nuisance as they bite through the line. Their only saving grace is their ability to inflate their bellies when caught and then blow a raspberry as they deflate, which always raises a smile. But then something big grabbed the bait and took me all over the place before it (and I) had had enough. It was a jack of about ten pounds – my biggest so far.

Talking of pufferfish, on a recent boat trip Jilly was in charge of one rod that had a sardine as bait, suspended from a big fat float. She yelled out that she had a bite, the float was bobbing. When we reeled in, we realised that a pufferfish had decided to see what the float tasted like and had used its razor-sharp teeth to bite chunks out of it. It looked like bites taken out of an apple!

Jilly, meanwhile, found a nice, gentle yoga class early in the day so she goes to her class and I go fishing, which works well. The other day a stray dog decided to accompany her as she walked to yoga and as she started the class, she noticed that the dog had come right into the studio and was curled up on one of the mats. She didn't let on that the dog was anything to do with her.

As usual on this island, time whizzed by and suddenly it was our last day. As luck would have it the tide was way out early that morning which meant we could do one of our favourite things, walk the sand bar. This sand bar is only exposed on very low tides and you have to time it right and walk out as the tide is dropping, then walk back before it's covered again. It adds a tiny element of risk to the hike, but it's so worthwhile. It took us three hours altogether and we only met about four other couples on the pristine sand. There were lots of different sea birds there and some nice shells to be found, but every time we found a big cone-shaped shell we had to leave it as there was still someone at home peeping out! On the way back the tide was coming in fast, so we speeded up a bit to avoid having to swim back to dry land. We spotted something flapping in the shallows which at first I thought was a turtle but on closer inspection it turned out to be a manta ray that flew off into deeper water when it saw us.

After a leisurely lunch at our apartment we took a golf cart taxi to Punta Coco and spent a couple of happy hours casting for jack whilst standing in the warm water. There was a lot of tide flowing so I only caught one, although it was a fair size and fought well.

Next morning we took the 7am ferry back to the mainland for a two-hour ride in a minibus back to Cancun. We dumped our bags in the left luggage at the bus station, then walked around the corner to a quiet pedestrian-only street where we had a long and lazy lunch at the same friendly restaurant we visited a year ago.

The BA flight home was peaceful and we slept a good part of the way before catching the train to

Swindon, where our daughter met us and drove us back to our poor, battered home. Whilst we've been away, we had it re-wired and also some internal construction done, so we were faced with a huge amount of dust, but at least the builders had done most of the messy stuff whilst we were absent, and it was nice to see the daffodils in flower.

Did we do too much? Was there too much travelling? The answer to both questions is probably yes, but when the hairdresser asks, "Been anywhere nice?" we can definitely say, "Oh yes!"

Afterword

So now I'm 75, but the journeys are far from over (I hope!). In a few weeks' time we're off on our travels again, and there are so many wonderful places to see – China, India, Thailand, Bali, Cambodia and Peru, to name but a few. With all those fabulous places to visit and postcards to write, it's just possible there's another book in the offing – who knows? They talk about Bucket Lists these days, but at our age perhaps Kick the Bucket Lists are more appropriate! But whilst we're fit enough there's every reason to keep on exploring this amazing world of ours – and that's exactly what we plan to do.

15851602R00140

0

 Printed in Great Britain
by Amazon